In Search of Stevie Smith

Florence Margaret "Stevie" Smith.
Courtesy of James MacGibbon.

In Search of
STEVIE SMITH

✳

Edited and with an introduction by
SANFORD STERNLICHT

SYRACUSE UNIVERSITY PRESS

54150

Copyright © 1991 by Syracuse University Press
Syracuse, New York 13244-5160

First Edition
91 92 93 94 95 96 97 98 99   6 5 4 3 2 1

The paper used in this publication meets the minimum requirements of
American National Standard for Information Sciences—Permanence of Paper
for Printed Library Materials, ANSI Z39.48-1984. ∞™

Library of Congress Cataloging-in-Publication Data

In search of Stevie Smith / edited and with an introduction by Sanford
   Sternlicht. — 1st ed.
     p.   cm.
    Includes bibliographical references (p.   ).
    Includes index.
    ISBN 0-8156-2503-0 (permanent paper). — ISBN 0-8156-2504-9
    (pbk.
  : permanent paper)
    1. Smith, Stevie, 1902–1971.   2. Poets, English—20th century—
Biography.   I. Sternlicht, Sanford.
PR6037.M43Z7   1990
828'.91209—dc20   90-9936
[B]   CIP

MANUFACTURED IN THE UNITED STATES OF AMERICA

Who and what is Stevie Smith?
Is she woman? Is she myth?

—Ogden Nash

SANFORD STERNLICHT, Adjunct Professor of English at Syracuse University, is a poet, critic, and theater director. His works of criticism include *John Webster's Imagery and the Webster Canon* (1972), *John Masefield* (1977), *C. S. Forester* (1981), *Padraic Colum* (1985), *John Galsworthy* (1987), *R. F. Delderfield* (1988), and *Stevie Smith* (1990). He has edited *Selected Short Stories of Padraic Colum* (1985), *Selected Plays of Padraic Colum* (1986), and *Selected Poems of Padraic Colum* (1989) for Syracuse University Press.

Contents

Illustrations

Contributors

Calvin Bedient has written about many modern poets in such works as *Eight Contemporary Poets* (1974).

Terry Eagleton is a leading Post-Modern critic. His seminal work is *Marxism and Literary Criticism* (1976).

D. J. Enright, the distinguished poet and critic, was awarded the Queen's Gold Medal for Poetry, as were Stevie Smith and Philip Larkin. His work, *Collected Poems,* was published in 1981. The title of his article is taken from "Valuable."

David Garnett was a distinguished novelist and editor as well as a mentor to Stevie Smith. His best-known novel is *Aspects of Love* (1955).

Mary Gordon is the author of *The Company of Women* (1981). Her latest novel is *Other Side* (1989).

Seamus Heaney is Ireland's most famous contemporary poet. *Selected Poems* appeared in 1980. His latest work is *The Haw Lantern* (1987).

Michael Horovitz, poet and editor of *New Departures,* was a personal friend of Stevie Smith.

Philip Larkin, Britain's leading poet in the post – World War II period, died in 1985. He, like Stevie Smith, was awarded the Queen's Gold Medal for Poetry. The title of his article "Frivolous and Vulnerable" is taken from *The Holiday.*

Hermione Lee has also written articles about Virginia Woolf, Philip Roth, and William Hogarth. The title of her article is from *The Holiday*.

Joyce Carol Oates is the author of over one hundred volumes which include novels, short stories, and poetry. Her latest novel is *Because It Is Bitter, and Because It Is My Heart* (1990).

Peter Orr has interviewed several writers and produced texts and tapes for the British Council.

Martin Pumphrey writes criticism and teaches at the University of Birmingham, England.

Christopher Ricks has also written on Milton, Tennyson, and Keats. He teaches at Boston University. The subtitle of his article is taken from Alexander Pope's *Peri Bathous, or the Art of Sinking in Poetry* (1727).

Muriel Spark is the author of *The Prime of Miss Jean Brodie* (1961) and many other novels. She has also written studies on Mary Shelley, John Masefield, and Emily Bronte.

Mark Storey has also written about Byron and John Clare, and he is a specialist on Irish Literature.

Michael Tatham lives and writes in Bedford, England. The title of his article is taken from "A Soldier Dear to Us."

Janice Thaddeus, poet and author of *Lot's Wife* (1986), teaches at Harvard University.

Stephen Wade is a poet and is the author of *Churwell Poems* (1987).

Jonathan Williams's volumes of poetry include *A Selection of Poems, 1957–1981* (1982) and *Quote, Unquote* (1989). The title of his article is taken from "Not Waving but Drowning."

Acknowledgments

Permission to quote from materials listed below is gratefully acknowledged.

Peter Orr, ed. "Stevie Smith." *The Poet Speaks*. London: Routledge & Kegan Paul, 1966, pp. 225 – 31. By permission of the British Council.

Jonathan Williams. "Much Further Out Than You Thought." *Parnassus: Poetry in Review,* 2 (Spring – Summer 1974), 105 – 27. By kind permission of Jonathan Williams.

David Garnett. "Books in General." *New Statesman and Nation,* 12 (5 September 1936), 321. Reproduced with permission of *New Statesman and Society*.

Mary Gordon. Preface to *Novel on Yellow Paper*. New York: Pinnacle, 1982, pp. vii – xiv. By kind permission of Mary Gordon.

Hermione Lee. "Fits and Splinters." *New Statesman,* 97 (4 May 1979), 652 – 53. Reproduced with permission of *New Statesman and Society*.

Joyce Carol Oates. "A Child with a Cold, Cold Eye." *New York Times Book Review,* 3 October 1982, 11, 26. By kind permission of Joyce Carol Oates.

Muriel Spark. "Melancholy Humour." *Observer,* 3 November 1957, 16. Copyright © *The Observer,* London, 1957. By kind permission of *The Observer.*

Philip Larkin. "Frivolous and Vulnerable." *Required Writing: Miscellaneous Pieces 1955 – 1982*. London: Faber 1983, pp. 153 – 58; reprinted by permission of Faber and Faber Ltd.; and New York: Farrar, Straus and Giroux, 1983, pp. 153 – 58. Copyright © 1982, 1983 by Philip Larkin. Reprinted by permission of Farrar, Straus and Giroux, Inc.

Terry Eagleton. "New Poetry." *Stand,* 13, no. 3 (1972), 71 – 74. By permission of *Stand* and Terry Eagleton.

Janice Thaddeus. "Stevie Smith and the Gleeful Macabre." *Contemporary Poetry,* 3 (1978), 36 – 49. By kind permission of Janice Thaddeus.

Martin Pumphrey. "Play, Fantasy, and Strange Laughter: Stevie Smith's Uncomfortable Poetry." *Critical Quarterly,* 28 no. 3 (August 1986), 85 – 96. By kind permission of Martin Pumphrey.

Philip Larkin. "Stevie Good-bye." *Observer,* 23 January 1972, 28. Copyright © *The Observer,* London, 1972.

D. J. Enright. "Did Nobody Teach You?" *Man Is an Onion: Reviews and Essays*. London: Chatto, 1972, pp. 137 – 48. By permission of Watson, Little, Ltd., licensing agent.

Michael Tatham. "That One Must Speak Lightly." *New Blackfriars,* 53 (July 1972), 318 – 27. Revised by the author, 1989. By kind permission of Michael Tatham.

Michael Horovitz. "Of Absent Friends." *New Departures,* nos. 7/8, 10/11 (1975), 12 – 19. By kind permission of Michael Horovitz.

Calvin Bedient. "Horace and Modernism." *Sewanee Review,* 85 (Spring 1977), 361 – 70. By permission of *Sewanee Review*.

Stephen Wade. "Stevie Smith and the Untruth of Myth." *Agenda,* 15 (Summer – Autumn 1977), 102 – 6. By permission of *Agenda*.

Mark Storey. "Why Stevie Smith Matters." *Critical Quarterly,* 21 no. 2 (Summer 1979), 41–55. By kind permission of Mark Storey.

Christopher Ricks. "Stevie Smith: The Art of Sinking in Poetry." *The Force of Poetry.* Oxford: The Clarendon Press, 1984, pp. 244–55. By kind permission of Christopher Ricks.

Seamus Heaney. "A Remarkable Voice." *Preoccupations: Selected Prose, 1968–1978.* London: Faber, 1980, pp. 199–201. Reprinted by permission of Faber and Faber Ltd.; and New York: Farrar, Straus and Giroux, 1980, pp. 199–201. Reprinted by permission of Farrar, Straus and Giroux, Inc.

Chronology

1971   Dies of brain tumor on 7 March.

1972   *Scorpion and Other Poems* published posthumously.

1975   *Collected Poems* published posthumously.

1981   *Me Again: Uncollected Writings of Stevie Smith* published posthumously.

In Search of Stevie Smith

Introduction

Stevie Smith was an elemental poet of love and death. Although she often wore the mask of comedy, the mouth of the face beneath gasped with a Munchian scream. She suffered from the arrogance of male privilege; the drudgery of thirty years of secretarial work that drove her to attempt suicide; the pangs of unrequited love; the loneliness and loss of friends resulting from her need to criticize, use, and expose them with sometimes savage satire; the dullness of a self-imposed suburban exile; the emotional cost of the probity of her work; and from a natural diffidence and distancing that she could only throw off when, late in life, she mounted a reader's platform to singsong her verse, dressed like a schoolgirl in middy blouse and short skirt. Most of all, however, Stevie suffered from her ambivalence toward faith. She was simultaneously a doubter and a believer, and ultimately she found her only savior and redeemer in the god of death.

In writing about Stevie Smith today, one must call her Stevie, not out of any sense of condescension, but because she loved the name and preferred to be called by it. Florence Margaret Smith reveled in the bit of autonomy and the flicker of an illusion of male freedom her sobriquet gave her. All who cared for her during her lifetime or have come to admire her since call her Stevie. As Stevie she was the subject of a hit London West End play by Hugh Whitemore and of a motion picture. Appreciation for her work and fascination about her life continue to grow.

The feminist movement and press have come to hail Stevie as a precursor for the expression of disaffection by modern women with the gender values and practices of Western civilization.

1

Stevie documents for today's women the not-so-subtle indoctrination of their sex towards self-ambivalence and self-estrangement ineluctably created by the dominant male hierarchy as a tool of repression.

Essays and scholarly articles on Stevie are appearing more and more frequently. Two full-length biographies are in print, a long critical study is in the offing, *Collected Poems* and two editions of selected poems are available, early volumes of her poetry are locatable, and her three novels are selling briskly. Stevie Smith is the most widely anthologized modern British female poet today. No collection of modern British poetry appears without a selection of her work and perhaps an example or two of her Thurber-esque drawings.

Yet despite the growing critical attention that Stevie's work is receiving, actually positing the "real" Stevie and locating meanings and values in her writing have become more difficult simply because her stream-of-consciousness prose and her poetic embryos are so widely and so variously interpretable that exegetes clash and contradict. Stevie has been called an essentially public poet employing prosopopoeia to address her audience in several distinct voices including that of a child; an adolescent; a bitter, cynical woman; a theologian; and a philosopher. She has been called a stand-up comic and an ironist, a lyricist, a confessional writer, a closet dissident if that is not a contradiction in terms, a satirist, and a Christian apologist. She has been described as a lover of animals and a hater of children. (Animals did not compete with her.) She has been called a masker and a revealer. In the ring ratings of twentieth-century poets, she has been judged a lightweight and a heavy. She has been proclaimed an airhead and an egghead. She has been accused of anti-Semitism and general misanthropy. She has been praised as one of the most musical poets of her generation, and she has been castigated for having a tin ear. She was clearly preoccupied with death, but she lived her life with enthusiasm, even glee. She imagined extravagantly. She was a queen of contradictions, and she yet bombards us with binaries. She was . . . well . . . Stevie.

The purpose of this book, therefore, is to reintroduce Stevie Smith to her audience, to present a selection of the most trenchant orthodox and heterodox commentary on her work, and to allow readers to find a personal Stevie in these pages as well as in her own signification.

Stevie Smith was acclaimed twice in her lifetime; first as a young, avant-garde, 1930s novelist writing in stream-of-consciousness fashion with the feminist sensibility of Virginia Woolf, and over twenty years later as the laconic, piquant, fiercely honest poet of the 1960s. Stevie symbolized the pain, the passion, and the zaniness of the time, as well as the frustration, the melancholy, the bewilderment, the rage, and the incipient revenge of contemporary womanhood; for the very same forces, wrongs, and awakenings that caused the women's movement to come into being had created the impetus for the poetry of Stevie Smith.

Stevie's life can be read in her work; and, indeed, her life was her work. Broken friendships, professional rejections, and personal losses were the building blocks in the arch of her achievement, along with her seriocomic ear, her intelligence, and her creative skills. But the keystone was her special sensitivity, exposed and rubbed raw by disappointment and loneliness. The youth of the sixties made her a cult figure. They responded to her vulnerability, her iconoclasm, her cynicism, her indifference to the male-female power structure, her mature woman's perspective on sexual relations, as well as her recognition of war and aggression as immature male games.

Stevie, however, always thought of herself as a conservative. Her religious affiliation was Church of England, and she maintained her membership even as she criticized Christianity and professed agnosticism. Stevie's psychological makeup included a large dollop of Victorianism. Although she found pleasure in her belated second celebrity and always enjoyed and longed for the heady company of writers, intellectuals, and artists, she found lifelong refuge in her suburban Victorian home on Avondale Road, Palmers Green, with her very Victorian Aunt Margaret.

Stevie worked diligently as a writer. She felt that an artist should get on with her work and not pay attention to her critical reception or developing reputation. Furthermore, she was always convinced that there was a place reserved for her in the history of British literature.

Florence Margaret Smith was born in Hull, Yorkshire, on 20 September 1902, the daughter of Ethel Spear Smith, herself the daughter of a successful engineer, and Charles Ward Smith, a handsome young son of an affluent shipping family, who wanted to be a naval officer but married and tried to settle down instead. Stevie's one sibling, Molly, preceded her into the world by twenty months. Florence Margaret was called Peggy. She was born two months premature and barely survived. Her childhood was sickly. She remained a small, thin girl and woman until the last years of her life, when she gained a little weight. She was just a little over five feet tall.

Charles Smith quickly tired of marriage; his business trips away from the family domicile extended, and in 1906 he abandoned his family and his failing business for a sailor's life. Ethel and Charles never divorced. Mrs. Smith continued to think of herself as married even though her husband returned home rarely and did not support the family financially. They scraped along on a small legacy from Grandfather Spear. Unable to continue to live in her home in Hull, Ethel took her children to London in the company of her unmarried sister, Margaret Annie Spear, hoping to live more economically and expecting to find greater educational opportunities for her daughters, who would have to make their own way in the world. The sisters found an acceptable semidetached red brick terrace house, 1 Avondale Road, Palmer Green, and made it their home for the rest of their lives and Stevie's too. Stevie called it "a house of female habitation." Her great aunt, Martha Hearne Spear Clode, also lived with them from 1916 until her death in 1924.

Stevie Smith spent a lifetime resenting the defection of her wandering, immature father. She also felt, irrationally of course, that she was the cause of his deracination of the family's security. His barely remembered departure and his rare contact later with wife and children not only provoked guilt feelings in Stevie but also made her suspicious of men and the validity of their commitments.

Educational opportunities were indeed relatively good for girls in the London suburbs. Stevie spent ten years in the private Palmers Green High School and Kindergarten, where she was a competent if not outstanding pupil. Her Edwardian childhood was marred, however, by severe illness when, at the age of five, she came down with tubercular peritonitis and was taken to the Yarrow Convalescent Home at Broadstairs on the Kent Coast to recover. She was in and out of the convalescent home for three years, and it can be said that Stevie never fully recovered robust health.

The little tribe of women was religious. They became communicants in the nearby Anglican Church of St. John the Evangelist. Stevie never left the church despite her later references to herself as an "Anglican agnostic." The hymns always retained their beauty for Stevie, and the thought of God's possibility made the universe less lonely. Furthermore, the church provided cultural and intellectual opportunities and activities as well as an architectonic for her later metaphysical poetry.

During the zeppelin raids on London in World War I, the women and children in 1 Avondale Road hid and shuddered. Stevie would experience air raids again in the next war. In the third year of the conflict, Stevie graduated from Palmers Green High School with a prize for literature but no scholarship for her next school, the North London Collegiate School for Girls, in Camden Town. Molly had won a scholarship and Mrs. Smith wanted the girls in the same school. Stevie was an average scholar at North London Collegiate, winning a prize only for scripture. Molly would go on to the university while Stevie went to secretarial school.

Only two months after the end of World War I, in January 1919, Ethel Smith collapsed with congestive heart failure, soon followed by gangrene in the legs. Her husband was notified, and he arrived on 6 February, just in time to watch his wife die and loudly demonstrate grief at the funeral. A few months later, forty-seven-year-old Charles Smith married a woman thirteen years his junior and together they began poultry farming. He apparently no longer felt the need to return to the sea again. Stevie never visited her father or his bride, and she rejected every effort at reconciliation.

After graduating from North London Collegiate, Stevie enrolled in a six-month course in Mrs. Hoster's Secretarial Training College in central London, and soon she began her thirty-year career as a secretary. With Molly at the University of Birmingham and then employed out of London as a teacher, Stevie lived on in Palmers Green with Margaret Spear, to whom Stevie referred affectionately and admiringly as the Lion Aunt. Aunt Margaret provided the most important personal relationship in Stevie's life. She was mother, nurturer, homemaker, and companion to her niece until in old age she became an invalid, and then Stevie lovingly and devotedly cared for her until her death in 1968 at age ninety-six.

In the early 1930s, while horseback riding on one of the London commons, some passing boys called to her: "Come on Steve," referring to a popular jockey of the day named Steve Donaghue and perhaps commenting on her small stature. A friend witnessing the incident began to call her Steve, and other friends changed it to Stevie. At home in the world of Palmers Green, she remained Peggy or Florence Margaret. In London, however, she was Stevie from then on. For her two lives, she not only had two different names but also two different personalities. In Palmers Green, she was a prim and proper, single working woman until her somewhat eccentric dress and behavior later on provoked some derision. In the business world, and later the artistic world, her personality evolved from an exploited, quiet, nearly invisible grind at work to an assertive forceful contributor to the London literary scene.

After Mrs. Hoster's and a first job with an engineering firm, Stevie became private secretary to Sir Neville Pearson, chairman of the publishing firm Pearson, Newnes, for which she would work for the rest of her wage-earning career. During slack times at work, Stevie began to write poetry. Her job was frequently boring, if not demeaning; there was a lot of making tea and going shopping to buy presents for the boss's wife. The writing of satiric verse was a palliative for Stevie, easing the passing hours of the long work day. Eleven years of writing passed before Stevie saw her poems in print.

Stevie was somewhat overwhelmed by her sister's intellectual development and academic success. Reading, voraciously and ubiquitously, and writing poetry helped Stevie to feel less of an intellectual failure. Molly became a Roman Catholic in 1928, and the conversion shook up Stevie and much disturbed the Lion Aunt, who perceived the conversion as a betrayal. So Stevie and Molly refought the Reformation. It was good for Stevie. The controversy kept her thinking about religion and forced her to develop and refine her metaphysics. Ultimately, Stevie concluded that Anglicanism somewhat mitigated the inherent cruelty and sexism of Christianity, while Roman Catholicism did not.

In her twenties, Stevie absolutely devoured books, reading a new one almost daily. She studied Wordsworth, Coleridge, Byron, Shelley, Keats, Mary Shelley, all the novels of D. H. Lawrence and Aldous Huxley, contemporary French criticism, Oscar Wilde, Franz Kafka, and Spinoza. She became a speed reader able to retain permanently nearly all she had learned. The reading skills served her well later on when she came to a second career as a book reviewer. Stevie specifically avoided reading contemporary poetry, believing that it would confuse her and prevent the development of an original and independent style.

Stevie's first trips abroad were two-week holidays spent in Germany in 1929 and 1931. On the second, she stayed with Jewish friends in Berlin and was appalled at the sight of a swastika painted on their doorpost. The event caused Stevie to think of the ominous side of the German character at the same time that she renewed her acquaintance with the man who would be the first great romantic love of her life, a man who strongly admired all things German.

Karl Eckinger, a German-Swiss graduate student, was tall, blue-eyed, highly intelligent, and two years younger than Stevie. They had met briefly in London and met again by chance in Berlin. He lectured to her about the virtues of German nationalism and the weaknesses of British decadence. All things German were superior. After Berlin they met as planned in London and had their intimate moments while hiking in the English countryside. However, Stevie tired of his intellectual bullying. It ruined the relationship. Also, Stevie wisely began to back away from the unfortunate prewar tendency toward a "fashionable" anti-Semitism among British intellectuals. Although Stevie's later remarks about Jews in *Novel on Yellow Paper* and in some poems and stories were often insensitive, especially when she was clearly alluding to Jewish friends, she was not an inveterate anti-Semite like Hilaire Belloc, and indeed she quickly denounced German barbarism. Her anti-German feelings, developed in the late 1930s, remained with her all the rest of her life. Karl, however, did force Stevie to think about political philosophy and to embrace fervently the democratic system in which she was born.

Stevie's second serious lover was Eric Armitage, whom she first met at a church social in 1932, just after her break with Karl and his return home. Eric was a tall, dark, handsome stammerer. They became engaged and were quite compatible physically, but Stevie soon realized that a marriage between them would not succeed. Each was too set in his or her ways. Eric expected a conventional stay-at-home, cook-and-clean housewife, and at thirty Stevie would not even begin to consider a life with that kind of drudgery. They parted amicably, and Stevie eschewed forever a deep commitment to a man. She had enjoyed sex. She continued to have many male friends, but the idea of a longterm, intimate relationship faded from her thoughts. It was just not worth the trouble. Stevie was not a highly sexed person. She did not anticipate the loneliness waiting in the middle-age desert of biological singlehood.

Attempting at long last to publish her poetry, Stevie sent a manuscript to a literary agent in 1934. The agency reader deplored the "snobbishness" and "ugliness" of the poems and also did not like the accompanying drawings. All in all, the reader found the poems to be of dubious literary quality. Stevie was thirty-two and unpublished. She had no literary friends to speak of. She worked a long day at a desk and took the tube home to the suburbs in the evening. The house did not even have a radio until World War II because the Lion Aunt did not like the racket they made. Stevie had neither influence, wealth, higher education, or the encouragement of a mentor. There was no reason to believe that as a writer she was anything but a dilettante, except for her own trenchant self-evaluation that convinced her that she had significant ability.

In 1935 Stevie finally found a sympathetic and prescient editor, the writer-critic David Garnett, literary editor of the *New Statesman.* He accepted six poems for publication. Stevie again tried to interest a book publisher in her poetry. Ian Parsons, a young editor at Chatto and Windus, admired the poetry but urged Stevie to write a novel. He felt that prose narrative was a better medium for her. Dutifully she obliged and turned out a manuscript in six weeks, writing both at home and surreptitiously at work. Stevie typed on the yellow office paper that Pearson's used for carbon copies. Struggling for a good title as she finished the manuscript, Stevie settled for the literal *Novel on Yellow Paper.* She submitted it to Chatto and Windus, but despite Ian Parson's entreaties, the manuscript was turned down by the senior editors. It was judged too unstructured and without commercial possibilities. Stevie was not discouraged, however. She immediately sent *Novel on Yellow Paper* to the publisher Jonathan Cape, who had read Stevie's poetry in the *New Statesman* and wanted a manuscript from her. Expecting poetry, Cape received a novel and published it 1936. So the rejection of a poetry manuscript led to the writing of a novel, whereas the publication of a few poems led to the publication of the novel. The scenario is pure Stevie.

As the novel went to press, Stevie started a sequel. *Novel on Yellow Paper* was widely and favorably reviewed. Critics were astounded at the ability of the then unknown writer to combine direct narrative address and Virginia Woolf-like stream-of-consciousness writing with fairy-tale devices, movie slang, macaronic cullings of Latin, German, French, and Italian, and highly intellectual philosophical discourse. Furthermore, despite the gallimaufry of ingredients, the story of the heroine Pompey Casmilus was quickly recognized as the basic, aimless odyssey of young Western women of the 1930s. The original critics little realized how autobiographical was this tale of a girl working in an office, who falls in love, travels to Germany, and returns to her suburban London home where she lives with an old aunt. Pompey's continual monologue is an explosion of discourses on those thoughts, ideas, problems, and values of primary interest to her generation: love, sex, men, marriage, abortion, friendship, work, religion, literature, art, suicide, and death.

Pompey, like her creator, is ambivalent about gender. She is glad when she is free of her suitor, Freddy, who has been too demanding and who has tried to control her; but she misses the early passion of a relationship and the comfort of committed love. Then and now, readers of *Novel on Yellow Paper* sense the controlled hysteria, the stifled boredom, and the brave stoicism of the heroine, proud of her womanhood, and angry over the pusillanimity of most of the other women of her time.

Despite the success of *Novel on Yellow Paper,* Stevie saw herself as a poet, not a novelist. She did not enjoy writing prose. Cape, meanwhile, pleased with the success of *Novel on Yellow Paper,* published Stevie's first book of poetry, *A Good Time Was Had by All,* in 1937; and it too received an excellent critical reception, especially for a first book of verse. Stevie's was a new poetical voice in British literature, distinct and original, uninfluenced by the younger major modern poets of the 1930s, Auden, Spender, and MacNeice. Periodicals now pursued Stevie for contributions.

The second novel, *Over the Frontier,* came out in 1938. It is a sequel to *Novel on Yellow Paper* in which Stevie's heroine and alter ego, Pompey Casmilus, has a hopeless love affair with a consanguineous cousin and suffers from despondency. Trying to take greater control of her life, she travels to Germany where she joins a band of conspirators, becomes a spy, lives dangerously, and falls in love once more. The novel's themes are love, loyalty, sexuality, and, of course, death.

What would have been novel number three, "Married to Death," proved a false start. Stevie abandoned it on the advice of her friend and discoverer, David Garnett. A second volume of verse, *Tender Only to One,* was published by Cape in 1938. The collection, a mixture of poetry, parody, and jingle, was also well received. Critics and other readers began to take special notice of and to enjoy Stevie's unique humor. Also, they were both astonished and bemused by her antilugubrious fascination with death.

In her late thirties, fortified by her literary success, Stevie became less shy and began to grow slightly eccentric in her behavior and dress. She expected her new friends to fawn and dote over her almost as if she were a precocious child. She began to wear clothes suggestive of a schoolgirl's, she played mischievous pranks, and sometimes she even spoke baby talk. In part, of course, her childlike behavior reflected a perspective on art that manifested itself in the deceptive ingenuousness of her poetry. The voice of the elfin child or wise adolescent bespoke a key persona in her poetry. The infantilism may also have been a Mozart-like nervous reaction to, and partial rejection of her new-found and completely unexpected fame. More deeply, Stevie may have been crying subconsciously for sympathy and comfort for the suffering from having lost father and mother. Whatever the cause or causes, the attention-seeking and child-costuming increased with time.

Many of Stevie's new friends were part of the literary left of the 1930s. She met quite a few communist writers and intellectuals, particularly those connected with Cambridge University. Stevie, however, remained unmoved by Marxism, and she also rejected cocktail party Freudian psychobabble. Rather, she remained staunchly conservative in politics. Her seemingly inherent Tory party and Church of England positions could not be shaken, and she spoke out against communists and fellow travelers both before World War II and during the Cold War. Nevertheless, in truth, Stevie was little interested in politics. She was, however, firmly against some things, like religious dogma, mistreatment of animals, and noise.

Over the Frontier was a prophetic book in that Stevie foresaw that the coming war would find millions of women in uniform. When World War II broke out in September 1939, Stevie attended gas attack and first aid lectures and then volunteered as an air-raid warden and firewatcher. The latter duty was extremely dangerous during the London blitz. Stevie would work all day, return to Palmers Green in the evening for supper, eat with Aunt Margaret, and take the Piccadilly underground line back to central London to fire watch all night in the building she was guarding. Sleep was snatched before and after alarms and raids. There was little sleep to be had for Stevie and most Londoners during the Battle of Britain years: 1940–1942.

At that time, Stevie was hard pressed for money. Her secretarial salary could not keep up with wartime inflation, and she never made a great deal of money from her writing. Therefore, she began a supplementary career as a book reviewer. Stevie also tried to get work at the British Broadcasting System, but her boss, Sir Neville Pearson, discouraged her, not wanting to lose a valuable employee during the wartime personnel shortage.

Stevie began another novel, her final one, *The Holiday*. She wrote during lunch hours, when the office was slow, and while fire-watching. It was hard and slow going for her, for she was not a natural novelist. Her stylistic inclinations lay toward compression and syllable-by-syllable weighing and economizing. *The Holiday* underwent a series of rejections and revisions for seven years until in 1949, Stevie found a new publisher, Chapman and Hall, willing to bring it out. David Garnett had urged Stevie to stop writing about herself, but basically that was all Stevie could do; so although Pompey disappears in her fiction, Celia, the heroine of *The Holiday* takes her place as a Stevie reincarnation. Celia lives with her old aunt in a London suburb, works at a boring job, and has a frustrating and unfulfilled love affair. There are many tears and much wringing of hands in *The Holiday*.

Although Stevie preferred *The Holiday* to her other novels, it is the least interesting and fictionally satisfying of them, almost devoid as it is of exposition and plot. Stevie spends an inordinate amount of time preaching negatively about British politics and education, the Indian struggle for independence, and the Soviet occupation of Eastern Europe. Struggling for additional filler, she gratuitously includes an unrelated short story. *The Holiday* lacks the brilliance, wit, and humor of *Novel on Yellow Paper* and the psychosexual fascination of *Over the Frontier*. It is probably just as well that Stevie and the novel parted company after *The Holiday*.

While working on *The Holiday* during the war, Stevie grew close to, and perhaps became intimate with George Orwell, whose later novels, *Animal Farm* and *Nineteen Eighty-Four*, shared Stevie's conservative, anticommunist views. Orwell was employed in the BBC's Bush House headquarters while Stevie was trying to get in the door there as a reader of poetry on the air. Some of Stevie's friends believed that she slept with the married Orwell, and she more than hinted at it herself. Stevie, however, grew very angry with Orwell, believing that he had actually prevented her from broadcasting her own poems on the Overseas Program, which he directed. Her vituperation was so strident that some of it may have been owing to an unexpected rejection at the end of a brief affair. She got her revenge. In *The Holiday*, George Orwell is satirized in the character of Basil Tate, like Orwell a veteran of the Spanish Civil War, who is in love with Tim Fox. The latter also has some Orwellian traits. Thus Stevie paints Orwell as two-faced, a narcissist, a split personality, and a homosexual.

Even though *The Holiday* was published in 1949, Stevie was really a prewar novelist. The ultimate subject of her novels is not male-female conflict, sexual politics, or self-pitying angst; it is the nature of womanhood in a time of transition, as women moved somewhat disbelievingly towards the beginnings of economic freedom and legal equality. Yet the great theme of Stevie's prose fiction is the concept that mid-twentieth-century Western women are paralyzed by the conflict between their sense of gender and their ambivalent, vacillating role in modern society.

In 1940 Stevie tried to get Cape to publish her third book of poetry; but they deferred at first on the grounds that her books, though favorably received by reviewers, had not sold well enough. Furthermore, some people in publishing felt that her work was too frivolous considering the grave events of the time. Finally, Cape relented and *Mother, What Is Man?* was published in 1942. These poems continued Stevie's exploration of her fears of both death and life. During the bleak despair of war, Stevie tried to discover, understand, and express the sadness, the beauty, and the good and evil in the complex human heart.

During the war years, Stevie grew closer to one friend and began a second important lifelong friendship. She first met the novelist Olivia Manning in the mid-1930s. Stevie was a bridesmaid at Olivia's wedding, and she sent her friend to Jonathan Cape with her first novel. At the outbreak of World War II, Manning was in Bucharest with her husband, who was employed by the British Council. Stevie volunteered to keep her friend up on the London happenings while Manning followed the fortunes of war in the Balkans, Egypt, and the Middle East. The Stevie-Olivia friendship was nevertheless a rocky one. Rivalry sometimes flared up between the two writers, and they both enjoyed gossip far too much for the good of their relationship. In 1971 when Stevie lay dying and Olivia was informed of her old friend's state, she said: "Well, if she's really dying send her my love." When Stevie was apprised of Manning's remark, she laughed.

The novelist Kay Dick, then an editor of *John O'London's Weekly,* became Stevie's friend in the war years and little rivalry existed between these two women. The friendship endured, and one result was Dick's book of conversations: *Ivy and Stevie: Ivy Compton-Burnett and Stevie Smith.*

With the war over, Stevie began to read her poetry publicly. At first she was timid. Her employer had told her that she lisped and read badly. But she soon grew to feel at home on the platform and to like the recognition and the stipends. She learned to chant her poems in her high, off pitch, school girl's voice, providing chance melodies from her recollections of folk tunes and church hymns.

On 20 February 1949, Stevie's father died in Kidderminster, Worcestershire. His second wife had died previously, and he had named Molly and Stevie as executors. The estate was worth less then 500 pounds. Stevie declined to attend the funeral, ostensibly because she was preparing to read a story on the BBC. She had her revenge on her father.

To Stevie's dismay, as the 1950s progressed, her poetry slipped from fashion. She had convinced Chapman and Hall in 1950 to bring out another volume of her verse, *Harold's Leap,* which treats the themes of running away, deserting, opting out, and letting go. The publishing house regretted the enterprise because the book sold poorly, even for poetry. Stevie believed that *Harold's Leap* contained her best work to date. With her literary career waning, she grew more and more unhappy as she entered her fifties. Aunt Margaret, approaching eighty, was beginning to require her care. Stevie came to hate her secretarial job; it was stifling. She wondered whether she could get a job somewhere as an editor? Significantly, she worked for a large publishing house that brought out, among other things, women's magazines; but apparently no one in the firm had thought to offer the successful woman writer a more challenging and lucrative position, one more worthy of her obvious talent.

Stevie was afraid just to leave the employ of Sir Neville Pearson. She had come to believe or had been conditioned to believe that she could not handle the fierce competition, perhaps with other women, in publishing. No old-girls' network existed to aid her. Internal and external pressures became unbearable. Chapman and Hall declined further publication, Aunt Margaret required more and more attention, reviewing was exhausting, the secretarial job seemed demeaning now. In April 1953, Stevie wrote her most famous poem, "Not Waving but Drowning," the most despairing piece of black humor in the canon. An arthritic knee condition was causing her constant, severe pain; and she was under medical care. On top of everything else, she fell into a dispute with the Inland Revenue. On 1 July 1953, calling on the god of death to save her, Stevie slashed her wrists at her office desk.

After rescue by her fellow workers and medical attention, she was sent home. The family physician advised her employer that she was emotionally unable to go back to work, and so she was retired with an ungenerous pension after twenty years at Pearson, Newnes. Even heavier reviewing was now required in order to make ends meet. As no one was publishing her poems, she would occasionally slip one into a review as if to remind the public that she was a poet.

At least now Stevie could write full time; and there were opportunities to visit friends when her aunt was well enough to be left for short periods with a neighbor looking in. Stevie labored mightily to find a publisher for another book of poetry. She had been writing with increased rapidity. Publishers, however, were either disinterested in her work or felt that her poetry was just too unconventional or were unwilling to publish her drawings with her poems, a condition she insisted upon. Stevie had come to believe that her drawings were an integral part of her poetry, serving variously as introductions to specific pieces, as explanations, or as wry deconstructive commentaries. Stevie never considered her laconic drawings as works of art or herself as an accomplished visual artist. She was in fact communicating in a mixed media, through two sign systems.

Finally, in 1957, after much vacillation, André Deutsch published *Not Waving but Drowning,* Stevie's fifth volume of verse, with the illustrations she demanded. In it Stevie takes great risks, walking the thin line between whimsey and profundity while forcing an outpouring of pain, sadness, loss, and despair into brief sentences, short snatches of dialogue, and handfuls of monosyllabic words, as if challenged to electrify those generally worn out, almost invisible signs of English into fresh vibrancy.

The critics gave the new collection more attention than they had given *Harold's Leap,* and all the comments were quite favorable. The world of letters was looking once more, and more seriously too, at the poetry of Stevie Smith. It seemed as if, at long last, Stevie had come of age; but in reality the age had come around to Stevie. Absurdism had come into vogue, and Stevie's work fit in with developing literary theories and strategies. New Criticism, which advocated an Aristotelian objectivism and valued the well-wrought poem in terms of its intrinsic relationships and aesthetic problem solving, was giving way to more phenomenological theories, in which the poem is taken from the critic and returned to the author as a manifestation of psychology and to the reader or listener as language to be responded to singularly. Close readings of texts began to be supplanted by listening to the poem, and, when possible, the poet, heeding sound as well as sense. For one generation, the poem, like the play, became a temporal process rather than a fixed bundle of signs. It was the best possible turn of critical events for Stevie.

The positive reception of *Not Waving but Drowning* caused elation, even rejuvenation, in Stevie. She had become famous again. To her surprise and delight in 1958 a publisher, Gaberbocchus, was willing to bring out a collection of her Thurberesque, captioned drawings, *Some Are More Human Than Others.* The next year, Batsford published her humorously captioned picture book *Cats in Colour,* somewhat reminiscent of T. S. Eliot's *Old Possum's Book of Practical Cats.* More and more frequently, the BBC requested Stevie to read her poetry and prose, and in 1958 she made several appearances on "Brain Trust," a popular radio program on which panelists answered listener questions and discussed intellectual, cultural, and political topics. The following year the BBC produced Stevie's radio play, *A Turn Outside.* Radio exposure on such a mighty cultural institution as the BBC vastly increased Stevie's public recognition and helped lead to the cult-like adoration of Stevie and her poetry in the 1960s.

That decade marked the triumph of Stevie Smith. Perhaps a factor in Stevie's sudden popularity with the sixties' generation was that her genius needed the impetus of eccentricity. As a cynosure, she won the ear and then the eye of the public. Her talent as a poet then took over and kept her audience enthralled.

Stevie's financial problems also disappeared in the 1960s. She had located an excellent financial advisor, Ladislav Horvat, who nurtured small investments on Stevie's part into an estate of over 23,000 pounds at the time of her death; some of which, however, was the value of the property in Palmers Green left to Stevie by Aunt Margaret. Sadly, Stevie remained prepossessed by money almost her entire life and certainly long after she needed to worry about it. She was quite parsimonious in the last years of her life. Like many people who were poor in childhood or who perceived themselves as poor then, Stevie was continually in fear of using up her money and having to be dependent on charity in old age.

Despite her professional successes, the last decade of Stevie's life was very difficult. In January 1961, she consented to an operation removing her right knee cap. She had been in near-constant pain again from the arthritic knee damaged years before while playing field hockey in school. Unfortunately, the pain returned after the operation, and she was only gradually able to recover most of the use of her right leg. In October she had an operation for a breast tumor that fortunately proved to be benign. Life with Aunt Margaret grew more difficult too. The old lady was immobilized by an arthritic hip, and so she and Stevie retreated to the confines of the second floor of the house, now woefully out of date in amenities. The plumbing and lighting and kitchen facilities were still basically the original Victorian. When Stevie could get out, it was to dash to a university reading, a poetry meeting, or a recording session at the BBC.

Paradoxically the world was seeking her. Poets like John Betjeman, Philip Larkin, Robert Lowell, and Muriel Rukeyser wrote enthusiastically about Stevie's work and wanted to meet her. The young and newly successful Sylvia Plath wrote to Stevie for an appointment but took her life before they could actually meet. Perhaps Plath found Stevie's relationship with her servant Death a tempting one.

In 1962 Longmans, Green brought out *Selected Poems*. The publishers allowed Stevie the opportunity at the age of sixty to look back on thirty-five years of writing poetry and select those she felt had special merit. Stevie decided to add new poems to the collection and these were pieces of primarily religious and philosophical expression. The voice of the lonely, cynical woman persona, however, remained in focus; but, understandably, the voice of the wise child fades into the background. In *Selected Poems*, Stevie also began to write more about the craft and the business of poetry.

The American edition of *Selected Poems*, published in 1964 by New Directions, won a huge new audience for Stevie. Attempts were made to get her to make a lucrative American tour, but she declined partly out of fear of the vast country, partly because her energy was diminishing, but primarily because her aunt's health was failing. Reviews of *Selected Poems* on both sides of the Atlantic now compared Stevie to William Blake, Emily Dickinson, and Edward Lear. The most astute critics recognized that Stevie was a unique voice in modern English poetry. Now she was being translated into German and French. Leading American periodicals like the *New Yorker, Atlantic Monthly,* and the *New York Review of Books* eagerly accepted her submissions.

1966 was a banner year for Stevie. Even old Aunt Margaret, who never quite understood or appreciated Stevie's work as a poet, was impressed when her niece won the Cholmondeley Award for Poetry. That same year *The Frog Prince and Other Poems* was published by Longmans, Green. Its central themes are humankind's relationship with a God who most likely does not exist and Stevie's growing absorption with death. The collection is more reflective, somewhat less whimsical, and much more story-poem focussed than the previous collections. Also, the child-voice persona is nearly extinguished. *The Frog Prince* was widely praised for its uniqueness and for the poet's ability to give herself unselfconsciously to that degree of personal exposure which is the hallmark of great Romantic poets.

Aunt Margaret Spear died on 11 March 1968 at the age of

ninety-six; Stevie was numb with grief. Her aunt had been her surrogate mother and lifelong companion, a great, warm, uncritical person providing structure to Stevie's life. The loneliness that Stevie felt as an artist working in what was essentially a philistine environment and that she also experienced as a woman pinned by ambivalence toward emotional and sexual commitments was now compounded by living completely alone. Stevie's friends tried to get her to leave the Victorian relic on Avondale Road or at least renovate; she refused. The house was the carapace of her emotional memory. It was her fortress and her cave. A sad distraction and a new duty came soon enough. In May 1969, her sister, Molly, had a stroke, suffering partial paralysis and loss of speech. Stevie quickly moved down temporarily to Molly's cottage in Buckfast, Devon, to help in her recovery; and when Molly left the hospital, Stevie commuted between Palmers Green and Buckfast. Stevie had a wide streak of nurturing in her, contrasting with the studied, Dorothy Parkerish cynicism.

Meanwhile, in America, Alfred Knopf published *The Best Beast* in 1969; it contained new poems and some that had appeared in *The Frog Prince.* The collection is heavily sardonic, macerating rigidity, cruelty, hypocrisy, and uncompassionate church doctrine. *The Best Beast* was the last of Stevie's books published in her lifetime.

That same year Stevie's popular recognition rose to its highwater mark. On 21 November 1969, she received the Queen's Gold Medal for Poetry from the hands of Elizabeth II. The stories of the actual event are many and varied. All appear to have been launched by Stevie herself. What seems to have happened is that upon learning from the palace that she was to be so honored Stevie repaired to the rummage sale at her church to purchase a secondhand hat for the occasion. Thus the tiny, nervous parishioner who yet dressed in a schoolgirl's jumper and wore a Peter Pan collar, whose hair was still cut in a 1920s straight fringe, and whom the wicked children of the neighborhood ran from, shrieking, "Witch! Witch!" was going to a private audience with the queen.

Stevie was too early when she reached Buckingham Palace, so she went into the visitor's gallery to buy some postcards. She told a policeman on duty that she had an appointment with the queen. He did not believe her so she went for a walk in the park. It started to rain, and Stevie returned to the palace, finally convincing the guards that Her Majesty indeed was expecting her. Shown to an antechamber, she had a giggly time with a lady-in-waiting and a handsome gentleman of the court. Led into the presence of the queen, she was given a twenty-minute audience. Stevie quickly became convinced that poetry was not the queen's absolutely favorite subject, and when Stevie began to recite details of an infamous murder case which she was writing about, the royal smile fixed permanently. Ushered out, Stevie then dashed off with her medal to a London restaurant where friends were waiting; and they all proceeded to get properly smashed. Stevie drank sherry and port and could handle the heady wines quite well.

The Queen's Medal was the last award Stevie would receive; but surely if she had lived longer there would have been many more prizes and then other honors. In April 1970, however, Stevie had a bad fall in which she cracked three ribs while reinjuring the capless knee. She worried incessantly and needlessly about money and tried to sell some of her manuscripts. She considered applying for a government arts grant. She began to give as many poetry readings as she could schedule, wherever they might take her. Sometimes her stipend would be as little as 15 pounds, with little profit after train fare. Often, however, she made sure that she would be fed; and long before, she had become a master at cadging rides to Palmers Green by car. Simultaneously, Stevie was writing poetry profusely and doing heavy reviewing.

In November 1970, Stevie again went down to Buckfast to stay with and to help her sister; but Stevie began to feel ill, lose energy, and become dizzy. She had conveniently scheduled several poetry readings in the West Country but she found it very hard to meet her commitments. Soon she was frequently near to fainting and often heard ringing in her ears. She had to clutch at furniture to keep her balance; and most frightening of all, she began to lose control of her speech and was soon stammering. On doctor's orders, she canceled a reading tour to Scotland.

During the winter evening of 6 January 1971, while at Molly's cottage, Stevie became extremely ill and had great difficulty in speaking clearly. A doctor was summoned and he ordered her to be taken by ambulance to Torbay Hospital in nearby Torquay, where for a week she underwent various medical tests. An X-ray revealed an abnormality in the brain, and Stevie was moved to the neurosurgery department of Freedom Fields Hospital in Plymouth for a biopsy that revealed an advanced, inoperable, malignant tumor. Stevie was returned to Torbay Hospital. She tried to keep up her professional affairs and managed to complete the selection of poems for *Scorpion and Other Poems,* which would be published posthumously in 1972. Friends came and quickly recognized that Stevie was dying. She was not afraid. She had lost her ability to speak. Her good friend and faithful literary executor, James MacGibbon, is certain that she tried to signal him to fetch her sleeping pills from home so that she could command the slave Death to do his duty quickly.

Stevie died on 7 March 1971 at age sixty-eight. Her death was not Roman, but she had been ill only a few months and most importantly for Stevie, she never became dependent on others. A funeral service was held on 12 March in the Anglican Church of the Holy Trinity in Buckfastleigh, Devon. Her body was cremated, as requested in her will.

Stevie's literary reputation had continued to grow. The playwright Hugh Whitemore's *Stevie: A Play from the Life and Work of Stevie Smith* was a West End hit in 1977 and a motion picture version of the play was produced the following year starring Glenda Jackson, who had read Stevie's poems publicly, and who had met and admired the poet. But Stevie's greatest monument and the present and future basis for appreciation and scholarship is James MacGibbon's edition of *The Collected Poems of Stevie Smith,* published in 1975. Virago Press has helped enormously by republishing all the novels in 1979 and 1980 and by keeping them in print.

Although Stevie Smith's first literary efforts were poems, it is important to realize that her original poetry emerged from her techniques as a stream-of-consciousness novelist. In the novel, she was a monologist, and as a poet she worked similarly. Her lyrical poems are personal, testy, biting, funny, silly, compassionate, cruel, sad, self-pitying, egocentric, self-critical songs. She preferred the simply, basic, monosyllabic words of easy conversation as the signs with which to encode her emotions and ideas. She worked neatly and economically, trusting sound to stimulate the reader to interpret connotation and color.

The three voices of Stevie's poetic persona evolve from the novels, especially *Novel on Yellow Paper:* the elfin child or wise adolescent, the cynical, depressed woman, and the stoic philosopher. With the passage of time and concommitant ageing, the proportions in the triad persona shifted, and the young voice faded, the woman's grew less strident, and the philosopher's superseded. In a sense, Stevie shifted her attack on British bourgeois, church-ridden, male-dominated, brutalizing society from the subversion of infantilism to the frontal assault of philosophical discourse.

Stevie delighted in reinventing and then deconstructing archetypal folk tales and myths told children. In that regard, she emulated William Blake's simple nature, shadowy mythologies, and metaphysical gifts. Nineteenth-century British poets, the mainstays of her early verse reading, echo in her work: Coleridge's transcendentalism and his ability to lose himself in a dream world, Tennyson's moral narrative, Robert Browning's dramatic soliloquy, and Edward Lear's technique of juxtaposing humorous verse with equally mirthful illustrations. Most of all, clear affinity exists between Stevie and her nineteenth-century American counterpart Emily Dickinson, with whose life, art, and metaphysics she identified. Stevie owed no debts to twentieth-century British or American poets. She did not read them.

She was deathly afraid of falling under the influence of Yeats or Auden or Spender. The only "late" poet's influence recognizable in the Stevie Smith canon is the long-lived A.E. Housman, whom she outwardly disparaged but inwardly admired for his classical precision.

Although Stevie satirized middle-class suburban life and values, she truly never forgot her neighbors in Palmers Green, envisioning them as a small but necessary part of her audience even as she studied and used their vernacular. A happy result of this concern is that one need not be poet, scholar, or critic to enjoy the poetry of Stevie Smith. She may be pulverizing us, but there is little ambiguity in the process. Even though it functions on many levels, Stevie's poetry always remains accessible.

Stevie did not identify herself as a feminist. Indeed, in her mother's generation she probably would not have been a suffragist. Of course she was a highly intelligent critically observant, vastly talented, sensitive woman. Like so many bright women of her generation, she longed for men to be fair, kind, gentle, strong, honest, and supportive, while believing that they were arrogant, inadequate, unfeeling, dangerous, and destructive. Her observations and experiences confirmed her beliefs. For much of her life, she tried to play the game according to the sexist rules of the time. She allowed herself to be exploited by the London business world, which was totally male controlled. She knew that her bosses' concept of employable femininity included service and subjugation. Like too many women of her time, she had few or no role models, so she was not able to cultivate useful professional relationships with other women. She saw herself as a loner, and worst of all she accepted the demeaning calumny that women, professionally and sexually, could only compete. Thus she fought her battle against male control alone. She remained passive outwardly. Inwardly she laughed, cried, seethed, suffered, and defended "self." It was not and is not the way to win. If she had been more clearly aware of sexual politics, she might have fought back differently.

From childhood on, Stevie was fascinated by death. She survived two world wars. She "lost" father and mother early. Her belief in God atrophied and finally expired. What was left to love and worship? The god Death remained faithful and firm like a lover or like a father waiting with open arms at life's end. Suicide was always a possible means to end misery. Within her stoic philosophy, that act was an intellectual, rational solution.

Although Stevie wrote a significant corpus of metaphysical poetry, she was progressively disillusioned by Christianity. She saw dishonesty in the churches, and she violently disagreed with the conventional construct of God as demanding, vain, jealous, revengeful, eager to sacrifice the innocent, and very masculine. Stevie set about reconstructing God through her metaphysics into a more sympathetic, less autocratic and vengeful diety. She allowed God his maleness but feminized him too. He could rule her universe, but it had better be through love.

Logically then, Stevie rejected the doctrine of heaven and hell. There is no afterlife, only welcome oblivion. She rejected the cruel belief in eternal punishment, as well as the story of creation, the idea that God could bargain for redemption by sacrificing his only son, the belief that scripture is divinely inspired, and the concept that good only emanates from the Holy Spirit.

Yet religion was so beautiful. How hard it was for her to be an agnostic. The preferred ritual of her Anglican church or even the Roman Catholic church could inspire enormously, and Stevie was ever ready to talk about as well as to write on religion. Perhaps, like most, she searched for answers never to be posited. If in the end she could not concur with the religious beliefs of so many of her fellow humans, she did understand, share, and love the human needs behind their religious drives. In her poetic vision, Stevie attempted to comprehend and redirect Christianity, to illustrate and redress the grievances of modern women, to protest the suffering that humans inflicted on animals, and to admonish God.

Stevie wrote without waste, always trimming to the clearest, to the direct, to the essential truth. One of the most musical of British poets, Stevie shaped her songs along Blakean lines: profundity through disingenuousness. She loved words but refused to be "literary." The world of Stevie Smith is as tight and as closed as that of Emily Dickinson, but it is also slightly askew, like a hat worn rakishly.

Stevie advocated endurance as the great virtue, expecting people to be brave and to fulfill life until they had earned death. She had fun. She loved her "nonsense" verse and the accompanying drawings. She could be wicked, sly, manipulative, vindictive, vituperative, and spiteful. She was hard on friends, using them as subjects of her satire, betraying their confidences, and exposing their foibles and contretemps. Then she would act bewildered when they protested; after all, did they not realize that a writer could only write from experience?

Stevie's poetry contains great transformations: a frog becomes a prince, a female secretary is drawn up into a Turner painting. The greatest transformation was not in her work, but in Stevie herself. Through her talent, intelligence, and hard work, all alone, the angry child, growing out from the suburban house of female habitation, evolved into a unique voice in twentieth-century British poetry and an indispensable model of candor, probity, and integrity in art.

The main body of this book is divided into four sections. The first presents two key interviews, allowing Stevie to speak for herself. The second offers essays on her work as a novelist, the third on her poetry. The fourth section is devoted to essays discussing the total canon.

Readers of this study probably fall into two categories: lovers and fans of the writings of Stevie Smith, familiar with her poems and novels and wishing to know more about her life, the sources of her inspiration, the leading critical opinions, and the estimations of her place in the hierarchies of literature; and new readers who have read a few of her poems, have become aware of her reputation in feminist literature, and have found themselves somewhat confused or perplexed as to what to make of the deceptively simple, iconolastic, seriocomic writer, the Charlie Chaplin of poetry, who makes them laugh, cry, and think, all at the same time. For both groups, *The Search for Stevie Smith* is intended as the guidebook to a world where animals are always good and people seldom, where angels try to understand humans instead of vice versa, where little girls are older and wiser than their mothers, where men are insufficient and women never learn that fact, where friendships are not fun and loneliness is the steady companion, where God is androgynous when He is at Her best, and where Death is humankind's best pal. In other words, here is the Baedeker to Stevieland.

Interviews

Stevie Smith enjoyed being interviewed. The attention was stimulating. The best-known interview is the one she did with her friend Kay Dick that became one half of Dick's book, *Ivy and Stevie: Ivy Compton-Burnett and Stevie Smith*. Two other particularly significant interviews are Peter Orr's 1961 piece and the poet Jonathan Williams's recollections of 1963, published after Stevie's death in 1971. Orr brings his skill as a professional interviewer to bear on his subject, while Williams presents a picture of Stevie through her own words and his warm reminiscences of her.

*

Stevie Smith

PETER ORR

ORR: When did you begin writing poetry?

SMITH: Well, I wrote one or two poems when I was a child, and then I had a tremendous period of not writing poems again until I was about twenty, I suppose.

ORR: Do you enjoy writing poems?

SMITH: Yes, very much indeed. I love it.

ORR: Is this the sort of thing that you would do even if they were not going to be published at all?

SMITH: Oh yes, you would: it gives you a wonderful pleasure. There's a certain amount of pain about it too, but hours and days can go by, one sort of throws it away and goes and digs it up and tosses it into the air and finishes it off or doesn't finish it off. Anyhow, I love doing it.

ORR: How do the ideas for your poems come to you? Do they come in the form of words, of pictures, of shapes, of sounds?

SMITH: Well, it's terribly difficult to say where one gets them from, and one feels one ought not to say in case one doesn't get them any more. It's like that famous line from Browning: "Where the apple reddens never pry." Sometimes it's an idea I want to get across very strongly like "Was He Married?" which is a theological poem, and I argue those points to myself and then I notice this rhythm coming into it, this strong beat, and then I try to make the argument in the poem. There are different sorts of poems, you know, the argument poems, the melancholy ones, the ones about death, and a tremendous lot about witchcraft and fairy poems, which I suppose are memories from childhood and Grimm's stories and the German fairy stories.

ORR: Do you find theology plays a large part in forming or deciding your themes?

SMITH: It plays quite a stong part, especially if I have been reading theology, and there are very strong other threads coming in too. I get inspiration from books, but they are always books which are not in the least poetical; I mean, they are books about theology or history which have nothing to do with poetry. But sometimes an idea will flash across one's mind from these books which may be a counterargument, but it would form itself into a poem somehow and that, I think, is what happens with a theological poem.

ORR: You've got a very strong sense of rhythm: I think this emerges very clearly in your poems. Is this something conscious or is this just something in your nature?

SMITH: It is something in my nature, I think. It is very, very strong, I know, and that's why I like reading my own poems aloud — and best of all, singing them — because you can't score a poem as you can score music, so you can't really put the accents on paper so that other people will inevitably read them correctly, you see.

ORR: So you do think when you are writing your poems of having them read aloud?

SMITH: Well, no, of reading them myself. I don't really want other people to read them.

ORR: But you think of the sound of them?

SMITH: Oh yes, very much: they are sound vehicles.

ORR: I notice that you like to put some of your poems to music, to well-known tunes. Why is this?

SMITH: Well, there again, the rhythm. I think if you can fix it to a tune you will be quite certain that other people will get the right rhythm. It's a way of making sure. You see what a suspicious nature I have! But I like, when I have written my poem, to make sure that if it ever is read by somebody else aloud it will be read properly. This may be very arrogant, you know: I mean, the way that another person may stress the poem, it might be better than my stress, but naturally one wants one's own way in these things.

ORR: Are you a good judge of your own poems?

SMITH: I don't know, because I never judge them. I don't think my poems have changed very much since I started writing.

ORR: Does this mean that your own attitudes haven't changed very much?

SMITH: No, they haven't changed at all, I think. One has one's thoughts about things and one takes great pleasure in these thoughts and in working them out. But I should be very surprised, for instance, if one day I said, "This is absolutely black" and the next day I said, "This is absolutely white."

ORR: Don't you think that more and more of our poets and writers today are concerned with problems of morality, even problems of survival?

SMITH: Yes, but I think all poems must be concerned with that and always have been at every age, surely. I am very concerned with that, though I don't mind much about survival. I rather like the idea of death, and I think a lot of my poems do treat of these subjects. It is like this man who I had a poem about. He took to journalism you see, to earn more money, as poets do quite often; and in the end he met his Muse in the form of an old gentleman and cuts his throat, murdered him, and then kept hearing these ghost sounds which he had repudiated and refused to listen to. It's a very modern situation, but it crops up all the time through human life, surely.

ORR: You don't feel that we are more conscious today of the world around us than perhaps our parents were?

SMITH: I think the everyday things impinge tremendously and always have, and the writer must learn to say no to them if they get in the way and are of a bore and a nuisance, like the necessity of earning money, the necessity of keeping one's family, of having children. These problems go on and they press most terribly, and the world of my childhood, of course, was split with war, too. So aren't we being rather unphilo-

sophical, parochial really, about this idea that life is so different today? We rather seem to pride ourselves like children saying, "Never have things been so bad." But they have been
much worse, surely, in the past. This is a sort of childish
boasting, I think — that we are in such a parlous state nowadays. I should think we are not really.

ORR: Don't you think, though, there is a growing consciousness
in everybody's minds with mass communication, television,
radio, and so on, that the world is too much with us?

SMITH: Yes, but it needn't be, you see. This is the terrible excuse
people make. They are free agents, they must learn to say no.
They are not forced to look at television, though I think it
would be foolish to say, "No, I won't look at it at all." I think
choosing is using human freedom. You know Morgan Forster
always said, "Connect, only connect." Well, I should say, "Select, only select." I would never refuse to look at the television
because I disapproved of television. If it was something I
wanted to see I would jolly well look at it. But I'd turn it off
when I began to get tired. I once saw *The Trojan Women* on television. I wouldn't have missed it for anything. Wonderful.
And so odd to have made Helen like a streetwalker, and to
have missed the key to the whole play. I mean, in the line: "If
these things had not happened to us, we should not be remembered." Not quite an antiwar slogan that, eh? You see, if
you say no to things, when you say yes you enjoy them much
more because you come fresh to it.

ORR: Do you find that you are influenced by the work of other
writers?

SMITH: Well, some of the past writers influence me. I think Gibbon's prose is absolutely wonderful and one clutches these
wonderful sentences of his about the early Christians when he
said, "For it was not in this world that they were desirous of
being either useful or agreeable." I mean those superb adjectives "useful or agreeable." Indeed, it was not an idea that
would have occurred to the early Christians. One gets such
pleasure out of that, you see.

ORR: Do you find this has any influence on your own writing, though?

SMITH: Well, it sharpens it, perhaps.

ORR: Do you find echoes of other writers in your own poems?

SMITH: Not conscious echoes, but I dare say there are a good many. I don't read the contemporary poets, really not so much out of arrogance as that I feel one ought not to. One will get the lines crossed and begin writing their poems, and they will begin writing one's own. But it's just as well everybody doesn't feel like that, of course. I like some of Byron's poetry very much. Especially some lines come into one's mind. You know those wonderful ones about the Athanasian creed in "Don Juan": "It illuminates the Book of Common Prayer,/As doth the rainbow the just clearing air." I like romantic, sad poems, you know. I love Wordsworth's "Idiot Boy"; I think it's a beautiful poem. I can't forget it, where she looks for him and he's riding his donkey in the moonlight through the Lake District. It's absolutely wonderful. Then I love some of those lines in "The Ancient Mariner." What a sustained poem that is! Not a single line is wrong, not one foot is wrong. It's amazing!

ORR: So you wouldn't consider yourself a typical example of a 1961 contemporary poet?

SMITH: No, not just 1961, perhaps. But I'm alive today, therefore I'm as much part of our time as everybody else. The times will just have to enlarge themselves to make room for me, won't they, and for everybody else. Being alive is being alive, and being alive now and not in the last century.

ORR: I believe that you are publishing a collected volume of your poems accompanied by some of your illustrations. Are these drawn specifically to accompany certain poems?

SMITH: No, they aren't. I just sort of sit and draw sometimes. I am not a trained drawer, you know. It's rather more like the higher doodling, or perhaps just doodling without the higher. But I enjoy doing it, and sometimes the dogs which come have such a look in their eyes that you can't believe that you've done them. And the faces that come!

ORR: They almost take you by surprise?

SMITH: Oh yes, yes. Some of these faces are indeed dreadful, and yet some of them are beautiful.

ORR: Do any of your poems take you by surprise?

SMITH: Some of the lines I sometimes start off with that come to me when I'm half asleep, they do take me by surprise. And you think, if you are in your workaday mood (you have almost the financier's side to you, you see, the stock exchange side, all that sort of thing which is extremely shrewd), and then these lines come to you when you wake up and you think "What utter nonsense, hasn't the Muse anything better to do than that, than to throw such nonsense about?" and then you think, "Well, you know, it's a gift," and then you play about with it and then this tremendous pleasure comes, and then you think of the drawings in the box and some of these faces and animals. The animals are so extraordinary! This child with a terrible look on its face! This one does not have a poem. I just wrote as an underline for it: "Eighteen months old and already odious." Then I did one of a despairing creature crawling out of the water and clinging to the knees of a larger figure. And the saying underneath: "Not everybody wishes for eternal life."

ORR: Do you attach much importance to the more conventional devices and disciplines of poetry? I'm thinking of things like the sonnet form, regular meter.

SMITH: Yes, I do, because I can't work without this sense of rhythm and meter and sometimes it will not go right. It has to be worked at and worked at. It may take years. In one case, I remember, I put the thing away. It must have been fifteen years ago I started that wretched poem. I did in the end get the line I wanted. As for the rhyme, I think that the English language is rather poverty-stricken in absolutely correct rhymes: therefore you must use these assonances and broken rhymes. And then they are beautiful, I think, whereas an absolutely close rhyme in English can become a jingle.

ORR: Do you find that you seek the company of other poets and other writers?

SMITH: I like company very much. Of course, I live rather alone, really. I live with an aunt who is ninety. I'm very fond of her, but we live alone, and most of my friends are in London and I am a little way out of London. No, I see my friends and I like them, but they don't, most of them, seem to be writers. Some of them are. I don't know many poets. I know some novelists. But most of my friends are just friends, and I don't really know what they are. They are married and have children, their husbands are barristers or something like that, lawyers, or civil servants. No, I wouldn't say I had a tremendous literary acquaintance. But when I do go to publishers' parties I do enjoy them very much. I like to meet writers. I don't know where they meet in London. I mean, they don't go and sit on the pavement cafés. But, of course, the pavements are so awfully cold. I don't know where they meet. I think you must be friends with them to begin with. You can't just go and say, "You are a poet, so am I, so I am coming to dinner next Thursday." But I think in France a lot more of the brains of the community, the intelligence, goes into the arts than it does in England. I think in England the intelligence of the country goes into the professions and government. And of course you might say for the country it is a good thing that it does, perhaps.

ORR: But do *you* feel this is a good thing?

SMITH: I don't think it does any harm. I think a poet should get on with his work and not be bothered what his status is in the community. In fact, they can be too spoilt, I think, and I'm not sure that they are not a bit too spoilt now.

ORR: So you don't think that the poet should occupy a unique or favored place in society?

SMITH: No, I don't think he should at all. I think he should be just made to get on with his writing: put in a room with pencils and pen or a typewriter; and then if his poems are no good, then he must just be thrown out, I think.

1961

*

Much Further Out Than You Thought

JONATHAN WILLIAMS

I do not much suppose that we shall ever
talk as of old, until we come to sit as
cherubs on rails — if any rails there be,
— in Paradise.

— Edward Lear

I remember once picking up a copy of a faded blue book of poems from the thirties in Bertram Rota's bookshop in Vigo Street, London. I asked Arthur Uphill, who was tending the store: so who's Stevie Smith? "Who's Stevie Smith?" he exclaimed, as though I had failed to recognize Queen Victoria, Dame Edith Sitwell, Gertrude Stein, Mae West, and Bette Davis all walking down Savile Row together. "Well, *really!* Well, really, indeed!"

I set about remedying this blushing ignorance as quickly as I could. I obtained all her books. I paid calls to Stevie Smith's house in Palmers Green and chatted over tea or sherry with the famous aunt, "The Lion of Hull." I had her to dinners when I lived in Barbara Jones's house in Hampstead. On 13 September 1963, we did the interview from which excerpts are used in the following piece. On two other occasions I taped Stevie reading her poems.

The last time I saw Stevie was at lunch at the Old Cheshire Cheese in Wine Office Court. The date was 5 February 1970.

Charles Olson's recent death was one topic of conversation that day. Another was my urging Stevie to have a look at Lorine Nie-decker's *Tenderness and Gristle,* then newly published by the Jargon Society. Now, two years later, my favorite women poets in America and England are both dead. But, Stevie certainly gave little evidence of age or illness that afternoon at lunch. She always suggested some kind of mildly discommoded bird — perhaps a jackdaw with a touch of *Weltanschauungangst* or *Zeitmerz.* Anyway, she promised to come to Yorkshire that summer and be the first poet to inaugurate my sauna bath. She asked: "Won't they burn you for a warlock in Dentdale if you have such a contraption?" I said: "No, Leeds United and Manchester United just bought saunas from the same firm in Birmingham, so it's ok. What's good enough for George Best is good enough for Dentdale."

In March 1971, I received word of Stevie's death while I was in residence at the University of Illinois. Arthur Uphill, ever on the job, sent the first clippings: the excellent obituary in the *Times,* plus tributes from John Wain, Douglas Cleverdon, and Neville Braybrooke. The occasion of her death made me ashamed that I had not managed to transcribe our interview and make the assessment of her work while she was still able to read it with proper chuckles and chidings.

What I want to do now is print parts of our 1963 interview; then consider what the work means to one poet and reader whose last decade has been made so much more pleasant by knowing this person from — not Porlock — Hull.

JW: While Aunt snoozes from all the sherry and lunch, let's sit out here in the sunshine and talk. Let's go back a long time. How about the first book of poems, Stevie?

SS: Yes, *A Good Time Was Had by All,* 1937. And those poems were written a long time before the book was published. I suppose I started writing poems halfway through the twenties, I should think. And then I had a whole lot and I wanted to get them published and I went to Chatto and Windus. I knew someone who was a sister-in-law of one of the partners. And he saw them and said, of course: "You must go away and write a novel before you've published poems." He also said (to himself, *sotto voce,* ho ho): "I'm sure they'll never come back." But, I really did go away and write a novel. He actually did want to take it, but he was only a junior partner and the others wouldn't, so Jonathan Cape took it eventually. And then I went on writing poems and Cape published the first three books. And that was the reason. I didn't like the poems very well. It was always pressure and pain. They reminded me of pain. I dare say the pain was no worse than anybody else's pain . . . No, there's not much recollection in tranquillity—there's fear and pain and disgust and dislike and all those rather negative things, and that's why I wrote that poem with the line: "Why does my Muse only speak when she is unhappy." The truth is the second line after that: "When I am happy, I live and despise writing." I adore almost anything else.

JW: Has it always been true?

SS: Yes, it has always been true. It is a fear of life. "For my Muse this cannot but be dispiriting."

JW: When you were writing those early poems, I have the impression you were very much on your own. Were you friendly with, or associated with, other poets?

SS: No, I never have been. I've often wished I was more. I think you can be too much in this world, but you can be too little in it, too. And, also, there are many points about the stresses of lines and the technique of writing poetry—I think it's rather valuable to be able to discuss all this with other poets. I don't know where they find a camaraderie in this country.

JW: Listening to your poems and granting my ignorance of most of current English practice, I come up with one or two things that seem to have determined the forms and style. The Anglican Church, obviously, has had a great deal to do with it all.

SS: Yes, that's true, especially with the rhythms, the rather simpler rhythms of the *Hymns Ancient and Modern,* those being tunes I often sing to. "Hymn to the Seal" goes to the tune of

"Soldiers of Christ, Arise!" or whatever it is. And when I sing it, it "feels" very well, but of course it isn't the tune! I sing one to the tune of "They Played in the Beautiful Garden." Indeed, that's the first line of the poem. It's called "The Warden." When I was reading some poems the other day, a man in the audience got up and said, "I guess I must be the only person here who knows that tune." So, I handed him the book and said, "Well, I wish you'd sing it, because I only get as near to the tune as I can. I have very little sense of pitch or tune." So he sang it to the proper tune. And then I said I'd sing it now to "my" tune so the audience could hear the difference. I did. The audience was kind enough to say that I had made a "different" tune, but a nice one.

JW: I particularly like the way you do "One of Many." This is literally intoned, isn't it?

SS: It tries to be like the *Gloria* chant, which I have always loved.

JW: Have you been more than usually involved in the Church?

SS: No. I was brought up in a very feminine household, of course. My mother was an invalid and my aunt came to look after us. They were both good church ladies. I think it meant a great deal to them. And my sister and I were brought up in the strict Anglican way . . .

And we had a wonderful Vicar, who had the superb name of the Reverend Roland D'Arcy-Prestons. He was a delightful man. It was a very much smaller neighborhood that we lived in in those days — it was a country place, really. I remember one day the Vicar was at the finance meeting with my aunt because she was on the church committee. And some man in the audience, the accountant, was reading out the accounts while the Reverend Roland D-Arcy-Prestons, up on the platform, started laughing. A doctor nudged him and whispered, "Hush, you'll cause great offense." The Vicar suddenly got up and said, "Oh dear, oh dear, I wasn't laughing at Mr. Snoot — I shouldn't like him to think that — no, I was just laughing at the thoughts that were passing through my mind." We rather enjoyed ourselves then.

JW: Was your childhood all here in Palmers Green?

SS: I've lived here since I was four; since, in other words, about 1906. That's a very long time. Aunt and I are the only people we know who have never moved . . . As I say, it was country. Odd, coming from Hull as we did, to London. We really came from the town to the country. To woods and trees. Very nice.

JW: What about nursery rhymes? Anything from there? Mahler says he only works on material he got before he was ten years old.

SS: Yes, certainly. Quite a lot. Because so many have these tunes, rather simple tunes, that are so catching. I suppose it is also, as Mahler sees, that one knows them when one is so young and vivid. "Boys and Girls Come Out to Play." "Oranges and Lemons." And then, the Brothers Grimm, of course. I love the fairy stories so much I still read them. And the rhymes you get!—like the Cinderella one, when she and the sisters tried the slippers on right away and the boys cried out: "Look behind, look behind, There's blood upon the shoe. The shoe's too small, The one behind is not the bride for you." They're very fascinating.

And there's another thing I always have read a lot of and really loved and that's the early nineteenth-century stuff. Coleridge and those poets. Oh, how I wish he had finished "Christabel"—how wicked it was to leave it unfinished. And *Vathek*—that's a story. I like Beckford very much. He wrote *Vathek* in French and then it was pinched by a friend of his, who translated it and published it as his own translation from the Arabic. It's rather maddening, all of it, but it's the last few pages, when they're all really in hell and in this vast palace. The light is simply too much, but they're given three days when they're quite all right, these three people. Then, everybody is rushing about, clutching his heart. Someone then explains: after three days your heart catches on fire and then it's on fire forever more. I love that theory.

JW: What about Mr. Blake?

ss: I don't know why, but I've always had the feeling one should be on one's guard there. It was almost "too easy." His are very easy echoes to catch.

JW: What about your contemporaries and some of the literary characters who think of themselves as much more "professional" than yourself?

ss: I honestly don't know, because I'm very much out of it. I don't know what they write. Again, I feel on my guard; I feel I might catch the too-easy echo. It's like getting telephone lines crossed—you get something through, but it's meant for another, not for you. Occasionally, I meet the people, and I like them very much, as people . . . Besides, we shouldn't forget the reviewing I do. You meet other reviewers, other writers.

JW: You do a lot of reviewing, steadily over the years?

ss: Not as steadily as I ought to. I hate the idea of having to, but that's just laziness.

JW: One or two of your pieces I've seen were reviews of mythological or theological books. Is that the kind of thing they send you primarily?

ss: Yes, that's what I like to get. It's so different from one's own life. I like the history in them. One I enjoyed recently was a classical dictionary by some Dublin don who had this great admiration for Achilles: "He was a true type of a gentleman." What an extraordinary way of putting it.

JW: I saw another review of a history of cats that you did.

ss: Yes, a horrible book. It was so cruel . . . These books that are supposed to be of such contemporary importance and interest —they depress me so. But I have a wonderful means of escape: I read Agatha Christie in French! I think she's a genius. If you read her in French you get a most exotic flavor, because there never was anything more English than the stuff she's writing. It's great fun that the translations are rather poor. Like where the lady companion in the original says: "Oh dear, oh dear!" And the French says: *"Mon Dieu, mon Dieu!"* She certainly *never* would . . . Aunt and I would, thus, always have something to talk about at breakfast on holiday. We'd come down to fresh juice from fresh fruit. Aunt would say: "Well, what about the expression 'poor as a church mouse?'" And . . . It's the tremendous power of taking weight off the mind, these books of hers have. You might say that any "light" reading has that, but it simply isn't true.

JW: Is Agatha Christie still writing?

SS: I wish she'd write more, but, poor dear, she *does* write one every year and hates doing it. Grinds it out for Christmas. I don't mind how much she hates it because it's really so good.

JW: I'd like to ask you to name a few other writers you like or have been influenced by. The other day I was talking with Mervyn Peake, and I asked him how many Gothic novels he'd read before he started work on the *Titus Trilogy.* He smiled and said he hadn't read *any* Gothic novels. He said the essential influences on his style, as he understood it, had been Herman Melville and Dickens.

SS: That's interesting. But, then, you never know how perversely a writer will derive his inspiration. For example, an author who spurs me to a lot of poetry is Gibbon. How very bizarre.

JW: I'd have guessed T. H. White was a man you liked?

SS: No. No, I don't like him very much. To me he doesn't ring true. I'm sure he's perfectly sincere with himself, but the books don't ring true—any more than Charles Williams's do. C. S. Lewis is, I think, a magnificent storyteller, but there are elements in him one dislikes intensely. Tolkien — the same thing. There was Charles Williams, whom they all seemed absolutely to adore. Talented men, but *something* rings false and is, in a way, slightly disgusting. If you want a good man on Arthurian stuff, then that's John Cowper Powys. I think Powys is the best man along such lines I've ever read. *Porius* is a magnificent book. It weighs about a ton and occupies one week at the end of the fifth century. I think JCP is a wonderful old man. I had a lot to do with him at one time. Did you ever read *The Inmates?*

JW: I've hardly read him at all. Henry Miller gave me *In Defense of Sensuality,* and I started the *Autobiography.*

SS: You know, I've never finished the *Autobiography* either. I often find that with Powys's prose. It takes a very considerable effort to read. You have to give yourself to it and work hard to concentrate. There can be exhilaration and enjoyment—if you're willing to make the initial effort. I remember when I first read *The Glastonbury Romance,* I didn't really enjoy it. The same is true of Ivy Compton-Burnett — you have to make an effort. She's wonderful. Most difficult stylists are difficult because they write badly. E. R. Eddison, for one, gives me all the pains, and none of the pleasures, of reading.

JW: You read more fiction than I thought.

SS: I don't really, you know. It's because I abhor the star-system fashions and all the novelists who play at that . . . I read DeQuincey. I like Evelyn Waugh. His *Scoop* is one of the best and funniest books I've ever read. One is terribly grateful for being provided with such pleasure . . . Another man whose novels I like — if I want to read a romantic novel about the upper classes, as sometimes one does — is Ford Madox Ford, although I think Maurice Baring is a much better author. They're joyful books. I think *Cat's Cradle* is wonderful.

JW: Have you plans for any more novels of your own? Yours seem stuck in amber, very ancient, like Connolly's *The Rock Pool.*

SS: How good Connolly can be. Poor man, he's stuck with reviewing all these years. It's a sort of bed-ticket for him and I don't suppose he's any more energetic than the rest of us. It's always the untalented who are so blasted energetic—publishing every day of the week and twice on Sundays . . . But, back to your question: No, I don't want to. I'm awfully afraid of novels. I'm afraid of what I say in them. I feel very queasy at the idea of having, for instance, *The Holiday* — the one you said you liked best of the three—republished. Nobody knows who one is, but oneself feels who and what one is *not*. I'd rather write books like Agatha Christie writes. There one gets out of the way.

JW: Are you out of the way in the poems?

SS: In a poem you can turn the emotions and feelings onto someone else, onto different characters. You can invent stories.
You'd think you could do that in a novel. Other people obviously can, and have. *But I can't.* The poem can claim to be
about a cat but it is really about you yourself.

JW: I wish you would make another selection of poems. There
were a number of vintage Stevie Smith poems missing from
the *Selected Poems.*

SS: It's difficult, you know, choosing.

JW: Well, just to name three: "Tender Only to One," "Come,"
and "Do Take Muriel Out."

SS: My poor publishers were trying to choose them all, and anything they chose I didn't like. And anything I chose, they
thought that wasn't right either. I'm amazed it ever got published. Anyway, I think I hear the kettle. We'll take some tid-
bits up to the Lion of Hull before she gets cross at all this literature . . .

Stevie Smith remarked (on another bit of our tape): "It's quite
easy with poems because you can carry poems around with you
while you're doing housework." So: poems, in the manner of
darning the socks . . . When not darning or poeming, Stevie did
a lot of doodling (her own word for it), "when not thinking too
much. If I suddenly get caught by the doodle, I put more effort
into it and end up calling it a drawing. I've got a whole collection
in boxes. Some are on tiny bits of paper and drawn on telephone
and memo pads. The drawings are not illustrations for the
poems. I take a drawing which I think 'illustrates' the spirit or
the idea in the poem rather than any incidents in it. When I look
through a pile of the drawings, I often am inspired to write more
poems. Lately [1963, this is] I like the drawings and I like to
gather them up into a book of just drawings with only captions,"
as in *Some Are More Human Than Others* (Gaberbocchus Press
Ltd., 1958).

The drawings, I must confess, are the aspect of Stevie's work that moves me the least. I can't find a cat in all of them to put with Mr. Lear's faithful Old Foss or one of Monsieur Grandville's curious felines. They're not even in a class with the stuffed pusses in Dr. Potter's Museum of Humorous Taxidermy, Bramber, Sussex. Nor can I find a single gawking female in terrible clothes and a lethal hat to compete with those of Mr. Thurber. I don't even yearn to possess a drawing by Stevie in the way that would make John Berger suspicious of my capitalistic, bibliophilic lust. The "Look, Ma(tisse), No Hands" approach to art rarely pays dividends in the hands of the amateur. Often Stevie Smith walked a tightrope in a poem where the eye could see no wire at all — and got away with it. I think we will just have to put up with the doodles, albeit wishing the memo pads had disappeared in the fire. (At this point a champion should rush to the fore, shouting: "For Christ's sake, the lady liked to have pictures with her poems. Let it go at that and don't be rude.")

Confessing to a further, mild rudeness, I say, well, they're better than the drawings, but I do not think Stevie Smith is going to eat much asphodel-pudding on the basis of the three novels she left behind. I can't possibly imagine how they read at the time — the early reviews were impressive. Stevie, herself, confesses to an overdose of Dorothy Parker at about the mid-thirties. I was going to Tarzan movies at the time and have never rejected them in favor of Miss Parker, so I wouldn't know. The style seems very much the Old Interior Monologue, come home to daydreaming on the Piccadilly tube-line to and fro from Wood Green Station, London, N. 22.

Novel on Yellow Paper (Jonathan Cape, 1936) is the first, and the only one people seem to know. *Over the Frontier* (Cape, 1938), the second, defies finishing. *The Holiday* (Chapman and Hall, 1949) is the most conventional. I used to think that Penguin ought to reprint *The Holiday,* but I don't anymore. Of course, this is where literary "criticism" gets so deadly. I reread those three books in five nights last week. Ian Hamilton Finlay was appalled when I told him this. He said: "Wait a wee minute, Jonathan, you must read only *one* Stevie Smith novel every five years—very slowly at that." He is probably right. In a triple-shot, they seem like nothing but chatter, chatter, chatter. There is no relief, and the prose runs through the ears like the salts of Epsom.

Still, if you can stand being the thrall of an art deco chatterbox for some considerable number of hours on end, do be Stevie's guest.

Last March I wrote to Basil Bunting about Stevie's death. He was in a snowbank in the wilds of Binghamton, New York; i.e., caught in the usual penal servitude of the academy ("I'm sick of universities—students *and* faculty!"). He wrote back: "So sorry to know I shant hear Stevie Smith again: little stuff, but honestly done, worked on." Mr. Bunting is not being haughty or dismissive when he permits himself to say only those few words about Stevie Smith. He is equally laconic about himself and gives us (somewhere in a reference book from Detroit about poets) a wry, five-word autobiography: "Minor poet, not conspicuously dishonest." Bunting abhors "criticism" of poetry, and so do I. Out of curiosity I've looked up *critic* in the recent two-volume microbiotic OED that is to be read only by stoned, myopic hawks. I like Thomas Dekker's warning in *Newes from Hell:* "Take heed of criticks: they bite, like fish, at anything, especially at bookes." (An even more scintillating remark has been made by André Gedalge, the teacher of Darius Milhaud: "Critics make pipi on music and think they help it grow.")

Before I have my brief say about Stevie Smith's poems, let me quote the very best thing that has yet to be said about her. It comes from an essay by Kenneth Cox entitled "Three Who Have Died": "Our own Stevie Smith, an English eccentric, riduculous and terrifying, aunt and prophetess, her voice between giggle and scream cracking the provincial vicarage, declaring again and again: There is no formula for poetry, no school, no authority, nothing but the spirit that moves and the wit and the nerve to give it utterance."

The operating word there, for me, is *nerve*. One might acquire benefits from exploring the technical mastery of the Baroque imagination of Edith Sitwell; or the etiolated, raspy line of Marianne Moore; or the backyard concision of Lorine Niedecker. The only interesting thing about Stevie Smith's technique is her cheeky, audacious lack of *any*. Granted, this legerdemain in legerdemotic style is very calculated and she comes out *original* instead of silly or stupid. (I can remember, to my discomfort, first hearing the Bruckner *Seventh* and wondering how anybody but a complete oaf could write a first movement with such an initial tune in it? Rédon used to put me into fits of schoolboy laughter. Pride goeth before destructions, etc.) In the Stevie Smith poem there is usually a touch from the Anglican Hymnal, a miasma from Colonel Blimp Land, something from under the stairs, something out of a ballad or the nursery. While Edward Lear— lovely and amiable man that he was — would welcome the company of Stevie Smith, it is not to be assumed that Robert Creeley, J. V. Cunningham, or Louis Zukofsky would welcome her to the region of their mordant, saber-toothed, strangulated poems.

Florence Margaret Smith, 1902–1971: quietly desperate, always saving, always drowning. Toward the end of her life, she said to Neville Braybrooke: "People think because I never married, I know nothing about the emotions. When I am dead you must put them right. I loved my aunt."

I trust that the Death of Stevie Smith keeps a spectral cottage near Kingston Bagpuize, so she can go to the pub where the Windrush meets the Thames and drink Black Velvets with Wordsworth, Coleridge, Pope, Shelley, Thomas Hood, and Dr. Sterne. Meantime, her cats Brown and Fry and Hyde will doze on their tombstones, while in the old woods there will be a "roaring peace."

1973

The Novels

Although Stevie never considered herself a novelist, it was as such that she first achieved literary fame. In the 1980s, the reissuing of *Novel on Yellow Paper, Over the Frontier,* and *The Holiday* excited great interest in her prose accomplishments, particularly with feminist critics and participants in women's study programs, where, quite rightly, Stevie's interior monologues are seen as gender documents testifying to the discomfiture, disappointment, and discrimination experienced by Western women in the interbellum years.

Reviewing *Novel on Yellow Paper* in 1936, David Garnett, truly Stevie's discoverer, immediately recognized the profound poetry in Stevie's prose. He also felt that Stevie could lead a generation of male readers to understand that they were measured and judged by women in the same way that they have measured and judged the other sex.

Mary Gordon, herself a modern master of the novel, notes that in *Novel on Yellow Paper* may be found the essential Stevie: all the qualities, values, and themes of the later canon, poetry and prose. For Gordon, *Novel on Yellow Paper* is a woman's life in its entirety. Stevie's vision is true, and her autobiographical prelections stifle the deep moan engendered by the prototypical, constrained, uneventful woman's life in Stevie's time and after.

Hermione Lee, reviewing the Virago Press reissue of *The Holiday,* recognized Stevie's sharing of Carlyle's apprehension concerning the apathy and general failure of intellectuals, the consequence of which is a weakened and demoralized nation. For Lee

51

The Holiday is a political essay as well as a case study of a woman's losing battle with despair.

Joyce Carol Oates, perhaps the most objective of major contemporary novelists, sees in Stevie's subjective novels the means by which the suburbanite secretary, Florence Margaret Smith, created "Stevie," as if her protagonists, Pompey and Celia, served as models for the eccentric, highly sensitive artist Stevie became. Thus the heroines of Stevie's novels are less autobiographical images than they are halves of reality, the existential doppelgangers of a pained and searching soul.

Books in General

DAVID GARNETT

Cutting up a silly book is the easiest part of a reviewer's work, and in doing it he can give all-too-convincing reasons. But the reasons one gives for one's likes always seem rather doubtful and farfetched. This week a book has made me happy for two days, and two days' happiness is not to be sneezed at. But what excuses can I offer for such a strange emotion? I feel sure they will seem unconvincing and invented. And first of all I must warn you, as the author will warn you, that it is ten to one you won't like this book at all, and then, thinking of my two days of happiness, you'll be raging with resentment and contempt. Proving yourself superior will be your only solace. Ten to one you won't like *Novel on Yellow Paper, or Work It Out for Yourself* by Stevie Smith (Cape, 7s. 6d.). But I like it; how I like it, and how difficult to explain why! It is written in a slangy, rather infantile jargon, with lots of Americanisms, German sentences, and foreign mishandlings of English; with Gertrude Stein repetitive mannerisms and tricks borrowed from Hemingway. But far from disliking this, I adore it because the result so completely expresses the author's character and gives pungency to her wit and her sense. It's like a lisp, or a stammer, which can add to the enjoyment of a joke.

> But first, Reader, I will give you a word of warning. This is a foot-off-the-ground novel that came by the left hand. And the thoughts that come and go and sometimes they do not quite

53

come and I do not pursue them to embarrass them with formality to pursue them into a harsh captivity. And if you are a foot-off-the-ground person I make no bones to say that is how you will write and only how you will write. And if you are a foot-on-the-ground person, this book will be for you a desert of weariness and exasperation. So put it down. Leave it alone. It was a mistake you made to get this book. You could not know.

Yet Miss Stevie Smith isn't by nature a foot-off-the-grounder, which is why I, who only like the *terre-à-terre,* like her. She has a foot-off-the-ground because she isn't writing a novel at all, but saying just what she feels about herself, her employer, her aunt, her lovers, her friends, and the good people, or not-so-good people, with whom she stayed in Germany. So her foot-off-the-ground is just a device for telling the truth which couldn't be told otherwise, just as the only way of telling the truth sometimes is by wild exaggeration.

That Lion, my aunt, has very sad late habits. At night time she has habits that are a genuine bit of Old Fielding. No light, late nightcap of Horlicks Is Helping Her Now, but the cold game pie she found in the larder . . . She puts the game pie on the table and finds in some remoter treasure trove a bottle of beer. . . . She props up the newspaper and reads from the legal columns. There is great joy there for my aunt, for there on the legal page Somerset House in all its black delinquency has been caught napping, has been found against by some despairing claimant . . . Sometimes my aunt reads out every bit of her income tax form aloud. With snuffling and sobbing in the throat, for the wickedness that is set down there, and fury in her old lion heart, and biting of nails, and thrashing of tail, up and down the house she goes, and scratching and scuffling round the house she goes to the cupboard low down where the receipt skewer lodges. Every receipt we have is impaled on this mighty skewer, and there is more rustling and scratching, and finally the receipt conclusive is produced, and now bursting with righteous triumph she sits down to write to James.

Then I must admit I agree with so many of Stevie Smith's opinions. She is always hitting the nail on the head. For example the neurotic condition of Germany gets on her nerves. First the parents slapping their child and telling it the story of Sneewitchen in which the wicked stepmother has to dance in red-hot shoes until she drops dead. Then the hateful feeling of a whole race giving itself up to dreams and cruelty. And when she has rushed back to England she thinks suddenly, suppose it were not a nation but an individual, this is what we should say:

> What is the matter with that poor Mr. Brown that has been looking so funny, he certainly looks queer, he looks a sick man? Oh, yes, where is that Mr. Brown that we don't see now, it is a long time, that was sick? Oh, yes, he was sick. Oh, yes, he got dictators, it turned out afterwards. That's what he got. Oh, certainly he was bad, very phony, very queer, but he got dictators like the doctors said.

There is so much I instantly agreed with, but which I could never have expressed for myself, that I naturally rejoiced over *Novel on Yellow Paper.* And since I agreed, I can't help saying Stevie Smith is an extraordinarily sensible girl. Whether she talks about Gilbert Murray's translations and Racine, about sex, or about being hopelessly and unsuitably in love, she always tells the truth and talks sense, and the slapdash pseudo-American slang acquires for me a strangely poetical quality.

> For two years now has Freddy been my own peculiar friend and playmate. But now he is proud, revengeful; will have marriage now or nothing, for he is in a huff, a puff of huff I thought that should disperse. But no it will not. Oh Freddy my sweet idiot boy, how can you be withdrawn so cold, so permanently huffish? You that had a loving giving face, a loving and inquiring charm, how changed you are, how different, how distant cold and dippy.

Men are always writing pretty things about women and don't need to convince us that they know something about love. But modern women seldom seem able to express a really strong feeling for anybody but themselves. Perhaps when things go really well they don't write at all, and it's the unsatisfied passions that get hammered out on the typewriter. Things have gone badly with Freddy too; but Stevie Smith shows that she loved him and not simply a reflection of herself. For that reason *Novel on Yellow Paper* takes the taste of a hundred best sellers, in which women value their lovers by the lengths of their motor cars, out of one's mouth.

1936

Preface to Novel on Yellow Paper

MARY GORDON

Like all genuine eccentrics Stevie Smith believed herself supremely ordinary. The setting of her life was willed, stubbornly, rebelliously: a choice of genius in the comic mode, of camouflage and self-protection. She lived in the suburbs with her aunt. There was much in her of the hearty, slightly hysterical spinster: sherry at four, hot drinks at ten, and witty drawings hidden underneath the blotter of the sitting room desk. Every word she wrote balanced between terror and hilarity. No writer is more death struck, and no modern has her knack of finding in the detritus of ordinary life such cause for mirth.

Novel on Yellow Paper shares the preoccupations of all of Stevie Smith: laughter, literature, death. It is a novel of nerves: it jumps, darts, turns, shrieks with laughter, recoils in horror, runs for a book, settles down to weep in quiet at the great blank cruelty of human life. It is the story of Pompey Casmilus, a young woman who lives in the suburbs and works as a secretary for a kindly publisher of women's magazines. Pompey's vision is unfixed and always shifting. Death, madness, grief peer over one shoulder, but behind the other is a sight so risible, a conversation so irresistable in its absurdity that death and madness, cruelty and grief must flee. At the end of the novel, Pompey is mourning her lost lover. She has decided that she is not right for marriage; that her rhythm is friendship with its comings and goings; that her beloved Freddy in his resolute small mindedness would choke her quite to death.

And I was lying in bed, crying with influenza and exasperation when into my bedroom came my Aunt the Lion of Hull. There was going to be a church bazaar. Auntie Lion was going to the bazaar dressed as a fan. Now all the ladies of the parish were going to the bazaar as a fan. But Auntie Lion was not at one with her fan. Standing in front of the double mirror in the bedroom she was making lioning faces and noises because of the obstinacy of the fan: Now it is fixed how do I look?

But the genius of Stevie Smith is not a serene one: it does not bring about resolutions, moments of stasis. No sooner has she enjoyed the sight of her aunt dressed as a fan, than she is overcome with love for her, and fears her loss. And, within a page, she tells us of her mother's painful death,

What can you do? You can do nothing but be there, and go on being there steadily and without a break until the end. There is nothing but that that you can do. My mother was dying, she had heart disease, she could not breathe, already there were the cylinders of oxygen. There was the nurse and the doctor coming day and night. But if you cannot breathe how can you breathe the oxygen? Even, how can the doctors help you. Or? You must suffer and then you must die. And for a week this last suffering leading to death continued. Oh how much better to die quickly. Oh then afterwards they say: Your mother died quickly. She did not suffer. You must remember to be thankful for that. But all the time you are remembering that she did suffer. Because if you cannot breathe you must suffer. And the last minute when you are dying, that may be a very long time indeed. But of course the doctors and the nurses have their feet very firmly upon the ground, and a minute to them is just sixty seconds' worth of distance run. So now it is all over, it is all over and she is dead. Yes, it is all over it is all over it is.

What a great deal of life we are taken over in three pages. The loss of young love, the hilarity of suburban manners, filial devotion, and suffering, the coldness of the objective vision, the finality of death. The comprehensiveness, the range, of this short

passage, its sheer interest, its felicity—all are possible only because the narrative voice is finely and deliberately controlled at
every moment. The seemingly throwaway *"well"*'s, *"and"*'s,
"now"'s, the parody diminutives, the quick, short repetitions,
are anything but throwaway in fact. They create the illusion of
the spoken voice; they capture the nervous aural genius of the
brilliant talker. It is a voice determined to take itself unseriously,
yet to speak of all that is most serious in life. It is a social voice,
a party voice. Above all, it wishes not to bore; above all, it wishes
to be amusing. For the speaker, Pompey, cannot keep out of her
mind—even as she tells us about funny clippings she has cut
from the Women's Pages—visions of horror, of cruelty that have
struck her with the terrors of the damned in hell.

She tells us she has seen the devil. Not for her the almost comforting fiend with its iconographic wings, tail, leer. Not, she
tells us,

> anything at all of the dark mind of Milton soaring up over the
> dark abyss, very damned and noble. No this was the fiend that is
> neither like Goethe's Mephistophles, that almost too impudent
> spirit of negation.

She sees the devil on the streets of Hythe after she is recovering
from the flu.

> Up on the hills by the canal, there were pieces of paper, and there
> were cartons that had held ice cream and there were those little
> cardboard spoons that go with it. And there were newspapers
> and wrapping papers.

> There was every sort of paper there, only the devil was there too,
> and he was not wrapped up in paper.

> It was a dreadful vision that I had there of the heart of this fiend.
> And every stormisch and sad I was too, and full of the black night
> of foreboding, and when I came back to the hotel I was very pro-
> foundly disturbed. Very horrified and bristling with the breath
> of the frightful fiend was Pompey.

The vision, it its very formlessness, its emptiness, its ordinariness, is the true heart of darkness. Papers on the street in a holiday town: the devil. The horror is real. And yet, Pompey's diction tries to make light of her horror; the jump into self-parody, the use of the swallowed whole German "Stormisch," the children's book inversion "very terrified and bristling with the breath of the frightful fiend was Pompey." Yet the horror remains. Yet it does not remain forever. There is so much to talk about. There is the list of funny quotations to bring out. We must be told the story of *Phèdre,* of the *Bacchae.* There are wonderful friends me must meet. And the important decision must be discussed: will she marry Freddy?

The pace of *Novel on Yellow Paper* is slightly frantic; it is marked, almost, by a determination never to be still. For stillness might reveal the truth that Pompey fears above all else, the vision she gets glimpses of: there may be nothing at the center, things may not be what they seem. She had her first glimpse of this possibility as a child, in a tuberculosis sanitorium when a nursemaid takes her on her knee.

> If I was in the mood for it I could play up to her fancy, but even while I was doing this I was immensely terrified. Her feeling for me, I felt this very keenly but could not for some time understand why it so much dismayed me, was in outward appearance, so far as being hugged and set on her knee, was what in outward appearance my mother . . . ? No, do you see, but it was profoundly disturbing, how in essence her feeling was so arbitrary, so superficial, so fortuitous. And so this feeling she had for me, which was not at all a deep feeling, but as one might pet, pat and cuddle a puppy, filled me with the fear that a child has in the face of cruelty. It was so insecure, so without depth or significance. It was so similar in outward form, and so asunder and apart, so deceitful and so barbarous in significance. It very profoundly disturbed and dismayed and terrified me.

It is then, as a child, that she learns to think of death as a friend, to reckon suicide a blessing and a comfort.

The voice we hear throughout the novel is a voice whose function is to cover over terror. Pompey is forever terrified; she feels at every moment her utter vulnerability, as if she were a burn victim, unhealed. She loves Racine, the Greeks, because they present the possibility of imperviousness. One is struck, time and again, by the central moral virtue in all of Stevie Smith's work: courage. For it is an act of the highest morality to swallow terror whole, to allow oneself to be distracted by the Lion Aunt, the advice in the Lovelorn Column, the fate of Phèdre and Pnetheus on the mountain. Pompey is self-absorbed, but she is not a narcissist. Against tremendous odds, she goes on loving life.

And so, *Novel on Yellow Paper* is a tale of heroism comically told, a heroism deeply modern: the triumph over the terror of the human condition. Stevie Smith has much in common, after all, with Kafka: the horror of the meaningless, the obsession with the ordinary details and routine of modern life. But where he falls into despair, she ends up laughing. The final vision of *Novel on Yellow Paper* is, to be sure, a vision of death. But it is the death of the tigress Flo, affronted by the insult of having been offered artificial respiration by the zookeeper.

> She looked, she lurched, and seeing some last, unnameable, not wholly apprehended final outrage, she fell, she whimpered, clawed in vain, and died.

But Pompey the tigress lives on. She cannot die just yet; she has much more to tell us.

1982

Fits and Splinters

HERMIONE LEE

The Holiday, first published in 1949, is a spiritual autobiography, a political essay, and an idiosyncratic exercise in poetic prose. Perhaps the closest thing to this strange amalgam is *Sartor Resartus:* and Stevie Smith shares further with Carlyle a violent irritation with hypocrisies and pretensions, a nagging solicitude for her country's state of mind, and a profound apprehension of the Everlasting No: desolation, apathy, "death-feeling."

Analogies with the Victorians can well be extended further. Stevie Smith is interested in Tennyson, and in the "dignity of suffering" which he allows his character in *Maud* and which we now find absurd and enviable. In much of her work there is a peculiar interplay between what she calls (in *Novel on Yellow Paper*) "loamish Victorian melancholy" and a stern aloof classicism. Tennyson and Greek tragedy are impressively grafted together in, for instance, "The House of Over-Dew," a dreadful tale of a gloomy Christian family life and lost love, which appears in prose here and as a poem in *Scorpion.* And the "plot" of *The Holiday*—Celia's sad visit, on leave from her postwar work at "the Ministry," to her uncle in Lincolnshire, with the cousin whom she loves but who may be her half-brother—has a mournful Tennysonian atmosphere of family secrets and damp woods.

But Stevie Smith's Victorianism is more than a penchant for Gothic families and Lincolnshire fields. Her religious anxieties seem markedly of the nineteenth century. In her novels and

poems, she was perpetually engaged in agonized conflict with
the established church ("Oh Christianity, Christianity/Why do
you not answer our difficulties? . . . the consolations of religion
are so beautiful/But not when you look close"). She longed to
embrace the solution, but it is "too tidy, too tidy by far." And the
vigorous, satirical authority with which she defines and attacks
the English character of the postwar years has, for all its topical-
ity ("England is a country given over to sloth"), almost an Ar-
noldian ring:

> We are not a sophistical people and are saved the dangers that run
> with sophism; and our education has not yet succeeded in taking
> away from us the weapons of our strength — insularity, pride,
> xenophobia and good humour.

These parallels with male Victorian writers may usefully work
against the more usual image of Stevie Smith as the fey spinster
lady of Palmers Green, all funny hats and pussy cats, which the
manner of *The Holiday* does in part bear out. Like *Novel on Yellow
Paper* and the poems, it is eccentric, abrupt, playful, and man-
nered. There is a good deal of English whimsy (like Auntie Lion's
dress with poppies all over it, which is called "Every One Came
Up") and a lot of weeping over the awfulness of life. But if the
quirky, freewheeling, "foot-off-the-ground" manner proves attractive rather than irritating, then *The Holiday* will yield up its
peculiar treasures.

It gives a clear, bitter picture of middle-class intellectual life
just after the war, and is remarkably good at political conversations—about India, about the effects of German propaganda on
the English temperament, about the social impotence of writers.
It's also a very funny novel with a caustic eye for office life and
suburban comforts, for the poisonous posh rich socialist who admires the countryside in terms of its painters ("One who always
comes back to the English school") and for the fearsome upper-
class London child:

"Did you and Bobby enjoy staying with Mummy?" asked the naïve school-mistress person. "Did we enjoy staying with Lois?"
poses the bored and shattered child, "perhaps rather, she drinks
a bit you know and Paul's cheque didn't come, but perhaps
rather, yes; we aren't supposed to particularly."

It's energetic in praise of independence, friendship (particularly
between women), and professional camaraderie. But it is, prin-
cipally, a document of suffering, a painfully close account (which
serves as an illuminating commentary on the poems) of Celia/
Stevie's battles with despair. The death wish is resisted; the novel
charts an honorable but tragic compromise: "Everything in this
world is in fits and splinters, like after an air raid when the glass
is on the pavements; one picks one's way and is happy in parts."

1979

*

A Child with a Cold, Cold Eye

JOYCE CAROL OATES

It is funny being like I am so tired, such a lot, it is funny, you can get a funny feeling out of it do you know. It is as if you weren't quite in focus maybe, it is like being a bit drunk, so you were lit up but still able to sit up and stand up and walk and smile, but it is there all the time, everything is shifted a bit the wrong way, like it was just a bit everything . . . *the wrong shape.* But very funny, very funny-peculiar the whole way along."

So the heroine of *Novel on Yellow Paper* muses to herself, by way of alleviating—or tabulating—the "orgy of boredom" to which her soul is committed: though the voice, the quirky, rambling, ingenuous, stubborn, funny-peculiar voice, could as easily be that of any other Stevie Smith heroine. In fact, Pompey Casmilus —christened Patience—is the narrator of both *Novel on Yellow Paper* and *Over the Frontier;* and the slightly more subdued Celia of *The Holiday* is clearly a close relation. And each chatty voice bears a close resemblance to that of Stevie Smith's own in her numerous essays, reviews, and BBC talks.

Since her death in 1971 at the age of sixty-eight, Stevie Smith has been honored by considerable acclaim, both in her native England and elsewhere. Her *Collected Poems* has been reissued several times; a handsome gathering of her short stories, essays, drawings, and reviews, *Me Again,* was recently published in this country, and her three novels, long out of print, have been reissued by London's enterprising Virago Press and are now made

available here through Pinnacle Books. Though differing in vir-
tually every other way from the late Jean Rhys and the late Barbara Pym, Stevie Smith shares with them a posthumous fame
that shows no signs of abating and is certainly well deserved. (It
might be remarked too that the film *Stevie,* starring Glenda Jackson, achieved a modest success in the United States and Canada.)
An idiosyncratic talent, invariably deemed "eccentric," very
much an acquired taste: a matter, it should be said, of tone, of
rhythm, of voice, that appeals to some readers immediately and
to others not at all. For Stevie Smith is all talk, all bright, brash,
forthright confession, and no pretense is made of larger poetic or
novelistic ambitions.

"Now Reader," Pompey interrupts her narrative to warn,
"don't go making trouble fixing up names to all this. I say here
there's not a person nor a thing in this book that every stepped
outside of this book. It's just all out of my head."

"Stevie Smith" is surely a character created by . . . Stevie
Smith, baptized Florence Margaret Smith, but later given the
nickname Stevie (after the then-famous jockey Steve Donoghue).
And the genesis of *Novel on Yellow Paper* is so whimsical it might
have been her creation as well: As legend would have it, she took
a manuscript of her poems to a publisher in 1935, was told to
"Go away and write a novel," proceeded to write it within a few
weeks (under the curious and not always felicitous influence of
Dorothy Parker) and managed to place it with another, more ad-
venturous publisher. Whereupon she achieved instant celebrity
in London's literary world. How droll, how marvelous — funny-
peculiar, as her wry voice would say. And the success of Pompey
Casmilus's tongue-in-cheek invention ("Does the road wind
uphill all the way? Yes, to the very end. But brace up, chaps,
there's a 60,000 word limit") is funnier than the thirty-four-
year-old novelist could have known at the time, since at least one
literary figure — the poet Robert Nichols — was convinced that
Virginia Woolf was "Stevie Smith" and wrote Woolf a somewhat
tactless six-page letter assuring her that *Novel on Yellow Paper* was
her best by far.

To an American reader in 1982, confronted with this garrulous, indefatigably quirky, I'm-just-typing-on-yellow-paper-and-associating-ideas-and-memories prose work of 1936, such a judgment, by a presumably informed person, seems preposterous. *Novel on Yellow Paper* is refreshing in its insouciance, perhaps, and in its refusal to attempt any traditional narrative technique; but the resolutely clever-talking voice never varies throughout the charge Stevie Smith made against James Thurber (that his tone and humor quickly became "monotonous") certainly applies to her. Initially, however, Pompey Casmilus surprises us with her directness, for it is quite as if we are given the privilege of overhearing private thoughts:

> Last week I was at a party. . . . Suddenly I looked round. I thought: I am the only goy. There was a newspaper man there and a musician and some plain business men. But the Jews. Well all to say about the Jews has been said, so I'll leave it. But then I had a moment of elation at that party. I got shot right up. Hurrah to be a goy! A clever goy is cleverer than a clever Jew. And I am a clever goy that knows everything on earth and in heaven. . . .
>
> Do all goys among Jews get that way? Yes, perhaps. And the feeling you must pipe down and apologize for being so superior and clever: I can't help it really my dear chap, you see I'm a goy. It just comes with the birth.

Pompey is a woman in her early thirties who works as a private secretary and lives in the suburbs with her aunt (the "Lion of Hull"). She has many friends, a "dippy" suitor named Freddy, and a briskly cheery attitude toward life, frequently undercut by observations on death. Pompey is primarily her talk, exclusively her talk, all chatter, all opinions, betraying now and then beyond the Dorothy Parker influence a numbing Gertrude Stein rhythm: "But first, Reader, I will give you a word of warning. This is a foot-off-the-ground novel that came by the left hand. And the thoughts come and go and sometimes they do not quite come and I do not pursue them to embarrass them with formality to pursue them into a harsh captivity. And if you are a foot-off-the-ground person I make no bones to say that is how you will write and only how you will write. And if you are a foot-on-the-ground person, this book will be for you a desert of weariness and exasperation."

And again: "For this book is the talking voice that runs on, and the thoughts come, the way I said, and the people come too, and come and go, to illustrate the thoughts, to point the moral, to adorn the tale.

"Oh talking voice that is so sweet, how hold you alive in captivity, how point you with commas, semi-colons, dashes, pauses and paragraphs?"

Novel on Yellow Paper is a gallimaufry of opinions on such subjects as Medea, D. H. Lawrence, Racine, Goethe, Christianity, and Nazism. It deals in its slapdash manner with "women's issues" ("And so thinking how everything is all right because she is married, and how she must not be anything but very gentle and kind to the poor friend who is still not having any man to wash up for, but is still awfully inferior and unmarried, she must be very tactful and kind to this friend, and not, oh no, she must not say one word to make worse for this friend the awful burden of inferiority, how her arms are empty, and she has no *kiddy*"). A story of some sort dimly unfolds in the background as Freddy disappoints: "And you my darling Freddy, my darling little child, my dippy Freddy, affronted, disgusted, outraged and reproachful. . . . There was never anyone as I who asked so much of nothing. Oh come on my darling Freddy and do not be so dippy," The chatter is occasionally sobered by thoughts of Pompey's mother's death and by thoughts of death in general. Like all improvised works, this literary curiosity strikes some inspired notes and others less inspired. Its value mainly lies in the fact that it was written by Stevie Smith at the age of thirty-four and that Stevie Smith went on to establish a distinct name for herself in poetry.

Yet if one looks for a self-portrait here—or in *Over the Frontier* and *The Holiday* — one is likely to be disappointed, for Stevie Smith rarely "sees" herself, and efforts at characterization are minimal. No doubt the narrator's claims for strong emotion are authentic, if we read Pompey as Stevie; but since they are not dramatized within the fictional context of the novel, they fall flat indeed. "Oh how I enjoy sex and how I enjoy it," boasts Pompey. But does anyone enjoy it with her? And what is one to think when suddenly the affable spinster-narrator declares herself a "desperate character" and a potential tiger "with claws on his feet that would go ripping and tearing the flesh"?

Punctuated with more somber ruminations on pain and mortality and on the "economics of Fatigue and Unrest," *Novel on Yellow Paper* fortunately assumes a less chirrupy tone as it approaches its 60,000-word limit. Pompey — or Stevie — speaks of her mother's difficult death and of her own longings for death and rises to a rare moment of lyric power in the novel's penultimate paragraph: "How profoundly impersonal is nature and how horrifying to the mind that is too little aloof, and yet upon no centre placed. To the heart of pain and the distraught mind, nature speaks only of death. Magnificent landscapes of the dream world, unfurling before the eye chasm upon chasm where no foot ever trod, and where the monstrous cliffs stretch down to an untouched sea, how often have I seen you from a distance and, drawn towards you, woken myself, to turn and dream again." But this voice of Pompey's comes to us from another level of being —from beyond the limits of the "yellow paper," perhaps.

Over the Frontier, published in 1938, continues Pompey's observations, but shifts, surprisingly and I'm afraid not altogether plausibly, to an adventure-espionage tale (or dream) that carries her "over the frontier" into war. (Pompey in uniform? This is her claim, which should probably be read as symbolic.) Like *Novel on Yellow Paper,* it is studded with small, quick, deft insights and perceptions; its thumbnail sketches of characters (like Colonel Peck, forever in search of his spectacles) will make it worthwhile reading for admirers of Stevie Smith but difficult going for others. Stevie Smith herself expressed considerable dissatisfaction with the novel in a letter of 1945: "It is horrible, I am so ashamed of it."

The Holiday, written during wartime, was not published until

1949 and was Stevie Smith's own favorite among her novels, though a contemporary reader is likely to find it too whimsical, too disjointed, too low-key to hold his interest except in patches. It seems to have served its author as a kind of daybook in which she could record passing opinions and memories, awkwardly linked with an ongoing "narrative"; but so uncertain is Stevie Smith as a novelist even her poetry suffers on this excursion: "Dr. Goebbels, that is the point,/You are a few years too soon with your jaunt,/Time and the moment is not yet England's daunt." And there is much more.

Stevie Smith wrote novels with the left hand and made no claims otherwise. She is justly celebrated for her remarkable poetry, which magically combines the rhythms of light verse (upon occasion, even greeting card verse) with the unyielding starkness of a tragic vision. She has, as Robert Lowell noted, a "unique and cheerfully gruesome voice"; and this voice is most skillfully expressed in short, tightly knit forms where insouciant rhythms can be made to dramatically serve serious subjects. One has only to read a few of her characteristic poems—"Thoughts about the Person from Porlock," "Away, Melancholy," the much anthologized "Not Waving But Drowning" — to fall under her eerie spell. Here is a childlike sensibility informed by a cold, cold eye and an inimitable, because poetically constrained, voice.

Nonetheless, it is good to have these three novels at last in print in the United States. And very attractively presented they are, with helpful introductions by Janet Watts and a graceful preface to *Novel on Yellow Paper* by the American novelist Mary Gordon.

1982

The Poems

Stevie Smith's poetry has had an excited, appreciative critical audience from the publication of her first book of verse, *A Good Time Was Had by All,* in 1937. The *Times Literary Supplement* then reviewed the book under the category of "humor," but other reviewers quickly perceived that Stevie's causeries were deeper than the surprise, the clever prosody, and the witty delights of the first reading presaged. By means of the disguise of verbal ingenuity, however, Stevie remains one of the most elusive poets of the twentieth century.

Early on, the novelist Muriel Spark was charmed by Stevie's use of chitchat phrases and comic metrical arrangements. But she soon grasped the central paradox in the work of the poet: that life is deplorable yet must be praised.

The poet Philip Larkin, an early admirer of Stevie Smith, first saw Stevie as a perennial flapper, but he was the first to recognize that her poetry stemmed from her novels, which are long personal monologues, while her poems are short ones. Later Stevie no longer seemed "freakish." Larkin came to see her as a consumate satirist.

Terry Eagleton recognizes that the straining for absolute honesty and truth is a primary characteristic of Stevie Smith's poetry. For Eagleton, Stevie's major subjects, particularly in her last works, were disintegration and death.

Janice Thaddeus sees the tension in Stevie Smith's poetry as between the child and the adult and between commitment and rejection. She finds a tonal oscillation between sadness and desperation masked by piquancy. Stevie's laconic simplicity is dif-

71

ferent from Blake's, with which it has often been compared. She has fun. She knows temporal joy. She makes us feel braver about life.

Martin Pumphrey describes the roles of fantasy, play, and "childishness" in Stevie Smith's poetry. Her imaginings and games serve to challenge conventional literary frames and unsettle the reader, who does not know how to "take" Stevie. She forces the reader to begin by deconstructing preconceptions about what is "serious" poetry.

The wide spectrum of ciriticism of Stevie Smith's poetry justifies a perception of Stevie as the great subversive of modern poetry, the double agent smuggling her carpet bag of intellectual, emotional, and prosodic tricks, disarmingly illustrated, back and forth over the frontier between art and kitsch. She is a mock mountebank selling profundity in pop bottles.

*

Melancholy Humor

MURIEL SPARK

This is the fifth book [*Not Waving but Drowning*] of surprising poems and Lear-like drawings by Miss Stevie Smith, who writes so differently from everyone else.

Her style is comic and her vision melancholy but dry-eyed:—

> Even as a child, said the lady, I recall in my pram
> Wishing it was over and done with. . . .

In the course of her work Miss Smith has created a poetic *persona* which she presents as a fantastic, somewhat blighted, observant and irrepressible soul, not so cheerful as you think, and "not waving but drowning."

The main theme of this collection is that life is fairly deplorable and yet must be praised. One of the most fascinating poems, "In the Park," portrays two old gentlemen walking by the lake, one of whom mournfully bids his companion to "pray for the Mute," whereupon the other, who is deaf, proceeds to praise the newt. "So two, better than one, finally strike truth in this happy song."

This poem is one of many half-hinted narrative pieces which better represent Miss Smith's talent than the shorter verses which frequently appear in magazines. She has a considerable range of forms: this collection includes some excellent ballad pastiche, some typical indignation-pieces against such things as

73

cruelty to animals and alterations to the Prayer Book, several chilly lyrics of horror and an interesting five-line compression of an episode from the Aeneid. Miss Smith's art is most of all dependent on the curious chit-chat rhythms, elongated lines, comic metrical arrangements, and mordant phrases which are used in this volume with particular skill and point.

1957

＊

Frivolous and Vulnerable

PHILIP LARKIN

Finding Stevie Smith's *Not Waving but Drowning* in a bookshop one Christmas some years ago, I was sufficiently impressed by it to buy a number of copies for random distribution among friends. The surprise this caused them was partly, no doubt, due to the reaction that before the war led us to emend the celebrated cigarette advertisement "If So-and-So [usually a well-known theatrical personality] offered you a cigarette it would be a Kensitas" by substituting for the brand name the words "bloody miracle." But equally they were, I think, bothered to know whether I seriously expected them to admire it. The more I insisted that I did, the more suspicious they became. An unfortunate episode.

Not that I blame them. I am not aware that Stevie Smith's poems have ever received serious critical assessment, though recently I have seen signs that this may not be far off. They are certainly presented with that hallmark of frivolity, *drawings,* and if my friends had been asked to place Miss Smith they would no doubt have put her somewhere in the uneasy marches between *humorous* and *children's.* She has also written a book about *cats,* which as far as I am concerned casts a shadow over even the most illustrious name. Nevertheless, her poems, to my mind, have two virtues: they are completely original, and now and again they are moving. These qualities alone set them above 95 per cent of present-day output.

75

Her mode of writing, broadly speaking, is that of the *fausse-naïve*, the "feminine" doodler or jotter who puts down everything as it strikes her, no matter how silly or tragic, in a kind of Gertrude Stein – Daisy Ashford – Lorelei Lee way. This method derives from her novels, those strange monologues (beginning in 1936 with *Novel on Yellow Paper, or, Work It Out for Yourself*) by a girl called Pompey or Celia, who works in some office or ministry, has childhood memories of the Humber, and at times breaks out into poems that are subsequently reprinted under the name of Stevie Smith.

I must admit I cannot remember a single thing that happens in any of them; but looking at them afresh I am struck now, as then, by the ease with which they skitter from "Phew-oops dearie, this was a facer, and a grand new opening gambit that I hadn't heard before" to "I feel I am an instrument of God, that is not altogether the Christian God; that I am an instrument of God that must *calcine these clods,* that are at the same time stupid and vulgar, and set free this God's prisoners, that are swift, white and beautiful and very bright and flaming-fierce." The accent of *The Holiday* (1949) is unremittingly artificial, yet the extraordinary scene at the end where Celia writes her uncle's sermon and begins to read it to him catches the attention in a way that suggests it is a key passage:

> There is little landscape where you are going and no warmth. In that landscape of harsh winter where the rivers are frozen fast, and the only sound is the crash of winter tree-branches beneath the weight of the snow that is piled on them, for the birds that might have been singing froze long ago, dropping like stone from the cold sky . . . The soul, frivolous and vulnerable, will now lie down and draw the snow over her for a blanket. Now she is terrified, look, the tears freeze as they stand in her eyes. She is naked in this desert, she has no friends, she is alone.

This is not the note of a comic writer, and it is a note that sounds throughout her work again and again.

When one turns to the "poems and drawings" (it is not easy to get hold of *A Good Time Was Had by All* or *Tender Only to One,* the prewar volumes), it is a toss-up whether one is too irritated by the streak of facetiousness (Kathleen ni Houlihan/Walking down the boule-igan/Ran into a hooligan" etc.) to find the pieces which carry the unique and curious flavor for which they come to be sought. There are, to be frank, a few poems in every book that should never have got outside the family. Nor do the drawings help: a mixture of "cute" and "crazy," they have an amateurishness reminiscent of Lear, Waugh, and Thurber without much compensating felicity. But one does not have to read far before coming on something that at first seems completely surprising (I was about to say out of place), as in "Dirge":

> From a friend's friend I taste friendship,
> From a friend's friend love,
> My spirit in confusion,
> Long years I strove,
> But now I know that never
> Nearer I shall move,
> Than a friend's friend to friendship,
> To love than a friend's love.

Or what about this from "The White Thought":

I shall be glad to be silent, Mother, and hear you speak,
You encouraged me to tell too much, and my thoughts are weak,
I shall keep them to myself for a time, and when I am older
They will shine as a white worm shines under a green boulder.

It is typical of Miss Smith that she sees something poetic move where we do not, takes a potshot at it, and when she holds it up forces us to admit that there was something there, even though we have never seen anything like it before.

> Do take Muriel out
> She is looking so glum

> Do take Muriel out
> All her friends are gone.
>
> Do take Muriel out
> Although your name is death . . .

Although *Not Waving but Drowning* (1957) was very much the
same kind of book as its predecessors, it seemed to me then, as
it does now, more confident, surer in getting its effects, than
they were. Its poems were less divided into "serious" and "silly":
as in Lear, the silliness was part of the seriousness.

With my looks I am bound to look simple or fast I would rather look
    simple
So I wear a tall hat on the back of my head that is rather a temple
And I walk rather queerly and comb my long hair
And people say, Don't bother about her . . .
                                     ("Magna Est Veritas")

As in "The Old Sweet Dove of Wiveton," poem after poem begins in her peculiarly plangent way, like a hand swept across
strings:

> 'Twas the voice of the sweet dove
> I heard him move
> I heard him cry
> Love, love . . .
>
> Put out that Light,
> Put out that bright Light,
> Let darkness fall . . .

Or, as in "This Is Disgraceful and Abominable," she can scold
remarkably like D. H. Lawrence ("Animals are animals and have
their nature/And that's enough, it is enough, leave it alone").
But she is always at her most characteristic when uttering the unexpected that once expressed is never forgotten. Her most celebrated poem, "Not Waving but Drowning," does precisely this:

Nobody heard him, the dead man,
But still he lay moaning:
I was much further out than you thought
And not waving but drowning.

Poor chap, he always loved larking
And now he's dead
It must have been too cold for him his heart gave way,
They said.

Oh, no no no, it was too cold always
(Still the dead one lay moaning)
I was much too far out all my life
And not waving but drowning.

Looking through this volume of *Selected Poems*[1] makes it possible to form one or two conclusions about this almost unclassifiable writer. It is impossible, as the blurb says, to date any given poem even to a decade, and yet one has the feeling she is improving — not, of course, becoming more consistent, for that is not her way, but dealing with stronger themes, having less to discard. Then there is the constant preoccupation with the concepts and language of Christianity—life, death, eternity, love, sin, all these are continually recurring in different contexts and from different angles. They do not make the best poems, but Miss Smith cannot leave them alone. It is not easy to judge her attitude to them. At times her tone is prophetic, as in "Conviction":

I walked abroad in Easter Park,
I heard the wild dog's distant bark,
I knew my Lord was risen again,
Wild dog, wild dog, you bark in vain.

But at others it has a kind of Rationalist Press sunlessness, as in "Was He Married?":

1. Stevie Smith, *Selected Poems* (London: Longmans, 1962).

> A god is man's doll, you ass,
> He makes him up like this on purpose.
>
> He might have made him up worse.
>
> He often has, in the past.

The language and history of the Church of England and its liturgy are in her blood, but so is doubt; in "Edmonton, Thy Cemetery . . . " she writes how:

> . . . Doubt returns with dreary face
> And fills my heart with dread
> ·
> And I begin to sing with him
> As if Belief had never been
> Ah me, the countless dead, ah me
> The countless countless dead.

And there comes a passage at the conclusion of the "Thoughts
about the Person from Porlock" that sounds as if it is as near as
imagination can get to faith:

> These thoughts are depressing I know. They are depressing,
> I wish I was more cheerful, it is more pleasant,
> Also it is a duty, we should smile as well as submitting
> To the purpose of One Above who is experimenting
> With various mixtures of human character which goes best,
> All is interesting for him it is exciting, but not for us.
> There I go again . . .

I stress this aspect of her work because it may correct the bias
of general opinion towards the view that she is a lighthearted
purveyor of *bizarrerie.* Of course her extraordinary jumble of
cats, knights, children, Racine, Excalibur, England and so on
gives some color to that view; but the truth of the matter is that
her talent is, as she translates Rimbaud's line, "drawn by every-

thing in turn." Almost anything can strike her, and she will have a stab at conveying just how it made her feel — a singing cat. Cranmer, Copernicus, fourteen-year-old girls, "The Occasional Yarrow" (a charming little poem, unaccountably missing from this collection), and thoughts and reflections that are hardly more than twists and grace notes of the mind such as no one else would ever attempt to put into words. And her successes are not full-scale foursquare poems that can be anthologized and ana-tomized, but occasional phrases ("not waving but drowning") or refrains ("For I love you more than ever/In the wet and stormy weather") that one finds hanging about one's mind like nursery rhymes, or folk poetry, long after one has put the book down in favor of Wallace Stevens.

> Why does my Muse only speak when she is unhappy?
> She does not, I only listen when I am unhappy
> When I am happy I live and depise writing
> For my Muse this cannot but be dispiriting.
>
> ("My Muse")

Perhaps this explains it. For all the freaks and sports of her fancy, for all her short pieces that are like rejected *Pansies* and her long pieces that are like William Blake rewritten by Ogden Nash, Miss Smith's poems speak with the authority of sadness.

1962

***

New Poetry

TERRY EAGLETON

If "superfluity" is one of John Berryman's chief characteristics, something similar can be said about a poet as different as Stevie Smith. Whereas, however, Berryman's superfluity resides in an excess of form to content, Stevie Smith's is the precise reverse: an ironic excess of content to form, a comic disparity between simple recalcitrant facts and the poetic shapes which try vainly to subdue them to precise, sophisticated uniformity. The carefully contrived bathos-effect in Stevie Smith's work seems to spring at least in part from this ironic determination to be honest to the facts at the cost of the form—to show how formal predictability is devastated by sheer truth:

> Mrs. Blow
> Loved her animals very much
> She often said:
> I do not know what I should do
> Without Hopdance and
> Clanworthy.
> They loved her too.
> > ("Mrs. Blow and Her Animals")

"Blow" just fails to rhyme with "do" and "too," and "Clanworthy" is formally a disaster—a disaster cheerfully underscored, of course, by being given a whole line to itself. The punctuation is chancy: no full stop at the end of line 2, but a

pedantically correct colon at the end of line 3, raising notably unfulfilled hopes of a weighty statement; and then the same device
repeated by the use of two full stops and a space to invest the
deadpan afterthought of the final line with a significance it is
comically unable to sustain. Another aspect of the technique can
be found in these lines:

> We said: She must have took him off
> To the forest old and grim,
> It has fell out, we said, that she
> Eats him in forest grim,
> And how can we help him being eaten
> Up in forests grim?
>
> ("Nor We of Her to Him")

Here, by contrast, "content" makes a stubborn effort to accommodate itself to "form," but succeeds only in effecting an
even more awkward dissonance. Preserving the meter means vi-
olating the grammar ("took," "fell") and displacing "Up" onto
the last line, with a consequent confusion of meaning; and the
whole tottering structure can be shored up only by an increasingly desperate grabbing at the poetic cliché "forest old and
grim," which rings ludicrously hollower at each frenetic repetition.

What makes *Scorpion* disappointing, however, is that its dominant themes prevent these resourceful technical devices from
being put to any very central use. The book, like Berryman's, is
really about disintegration and death; and the intensities it
touches on are difficult to accommodate in the language of nursery rhyme, "metaphysical" though that form can be in Stevie
Smith's hands. The poems, accordingly, tend to divide between
children's tales which intimate, but rarely explicate, a deeper
meaning, and more direct addresses which are poignant but
slight.

1972

＊

Stevie Smith and the Gleeful Macabre

JANICE THADDEUS

Florence Margaret Smith, who retained her nickname Stevie throughout her adulthood and published under its androgynous rubric, reveled in incongruities. Her poetic speakers shift from male to female, conformist to nonconformist, simple to complex, and adult to child; at times, indeed they are both alive and dead. She frequently set her poems to well-known tunes and sang them rather tonelessly to willing listeners, and she often appended sketches whose relationship to the text is problematical. Her syntax is odd, her rhymes unexpected, her numbers idiosyncratic, and as a result her work is nearly always lively and original. Her poems have an immediate appeal, and yet many of them bear considerable rereading. The frequent incongruities chiefly account for this double effect.

Smith's odd juxtapositions and her love of paradox invite comparison—not infrequently pursued by her critics—to Blake. She herself was aware of the parallel, even calling one of her poems "Little Boy Lost." Like Blake she writes parables, redefines Christianity, addresses animals, sees angels, uses simple language, and illustrates her poetry, but in all essentials she and Blake are significantly different. Blake's is a handy-dandy world where justice and thief change places, and so is Stevie Smith's; but Blake's humor is rarer and more likely to serve an ultimate if not an ulterior purpose. Smith's humor is embodied and pervasive, more like the sort of extra joy which Coleridge called the "blossom of the nettle."

84

Blake herds us through the London streets pointing out "Marks of weakness, marks of woe," and — lest we might not make the connection — attributes most human ills to mental slavery, "Mind-forged manacles." Smith describes the suburbs in equally unflattering terms in "The Suburban Classes.":

> There is far too much of the suburban classes
> Spiritually not geographically speaking. They're asses.
> Menacing the greatness of our beloved England, they lie
> Propagating their kind in an eightroomed style.
> Now I have a plan which I will enfold
> (There's this to be said for them, they do as they're told)
> Then tell them their country's in mortal peril
> They believed it before and again will not cavil
> Put it in caption form firm and slick
> If they see it in print it is bound to stick:
> "Your King and your Country need you Dead"
> You see the idea? Well, let it spread.
> Have a suitable drug under string and label
> Free for every Registered Reader's table.
> For the rest of the gang who are not patriotic
> I've another appeal they'll discover hypnotic:
> Tell them it's smart to be dead and won't hurt
> And they'll gobble up drug as they gobble up dirt.[1]

What Stevie Smith has added to the mind-forged manacles is what I designate "the gleeful macabre." When one thinks of the recent mass deaths in Guyana, this poem takes on a terrifying reality, but in the 1930s its initial assumption—that people will commit suicide for abstractions as heady as patriotism and as sleasy as fashionableness — was sufficiently incongruous to be funny. In spite of Reverend Jones and mass suicide, the poem still is funny. Indulging briefly in what Bergson called "a momentary

1. *The Collected Poems of Stevie Smith* (New York: Oxford Univ. Press, 1976), 26. Subsequent references will be cited parenthetically in the text of this article.

anaesthesia of the heart,"[2] some of us would happily see the sub-urbs thus emptied and cleansed of the manacled minds we despise.

Death, both natural and induced, was Stevie Smith's primary subject, at least partly because she knew that she could rivet an audience with it. In 1970, when the Queen gave her a medal, "the poor darling kept asking me questions about poetry. I rather got the impression it wasn't her favorite subject . . . and I got rather nervous and said, "I don't know why, but I seem to have written rather a lot about murder lately," . . . and the smile got rather fixed.' "[3] Stevie Smith's humor often — and quite de-liberately — evokes the fixed smile and the nervous giggle.

Her interest in death was not a pose. Her central assumption, the core of her nature, was the recognition that death is always available, the only friend who is as close as the river, waiting in every bottle of aspirin: " 'two hundred and I am freed,'/He said, 'from anxiety' " (*CP*, 197). Death was "end and remedy" (*CP*, 368); "I cannot help but like Oblivion better/Than being a hu-man heart and human creature" (*CP*, 562). Even in a 1970 an-thology for children, Smith mentioned in her introduction the freeing knowledge that death is available; and she chose to in-clude the "fiercer" romantic efforts, together with Blake's sick rose and Nashe's falling brightness.[4] Predictably, her American publishers insisted on publishing the book as an adult anthology.

We are all familiar with twentieth-century poetry which ex-alts suicide, especially poetry by women. But the feeling in Stevie Smith is quite different from that in Sylvia Plath and Anne Sexton. Plath's "Lady Lazarus" is clenched in anger and pain: "I do it so it feels like hell."[5] Sexton's death wish is egotistical, witchlike, six-fingered. Smith's suicidal speakers are more se-

2. Henri Bergson, "Laughter," in *Comedy: An Essay on Comedy* (Garden City, N.Y.: Doubleday, 1956), 64.

3. Kay Dick, *Ivy and Stevie* (London: Duckworth, 1971), 52.

4. *The Batsford Book of Children's Verse* (London: Batsfora, 1970), 3.

5. *Ariel* (New York: Harper and Row, 1966), 7.

rene, severed from the poet herself by the fact that they are almost invariably male. Although they are sometimes trivial or
absurd, they do not rake and claw their friends and lovers as they
go, and death itself is a gentle alternative to the complexities of
life — "Those sweet seas that deepen are my destiny/And must
come even if not soon" (*CP,* 562).

Being always ready for death requires a special kind of life.
Smith herself said, "I love life. I adore it, but only because I keep
myself well on the edge. I wouldn't commit myself to anything.
I can always get out if I want to."[6] Rejection and withdrawal, a
diffidence in commitment — these are often the subjects of the
poems. Affection is not simply spread around as in Donne's "I
can love both fair and brown"; rather, there is a general hesita-
tion. This gingerliness is the quality which perhaps most se-
verely distinguishes Smith's content from Blake's.

Rejection in Stevie Smith's poems can start early and continue
long. Even a three-year-old child can smash all the clichés of
commitment:

> My mother was a romantic girl
> So she had to marry a man with his hair in curl
> Who subsequently became my unrespected papa,
> But that was a long time ago now.
>
> What folly it is that daughters are always supposed to be
> In love with papa. It wasn't the case with me
> I couldn't take to him at all
> But he took to me
> What a sad fate to befall
> A child of three.
>
> I sat upright in my baby carriage
> And wished mama hadn't made such a foolish marriage.
> I tried to hide it but it showed in my eyes unfortunately
> And a fortnight later papa ran away to sea.

6. Dick, *Ivy,* 44–45.

> He used to come home on leave
> It was always the same
> I could not grieve
> But I think I was somewhat to blame.
>
> ("Papa Love Baby," *CP,* 16)

(Incidentally, this represents to some degree the way Stevie Smith felt about her own father, although she had to revise her opinion later when her mother died and he married a woman who called him "Tootles." Her comment on this was, "Well, if he can inspire someone to call him Tootles, there must be things about him I don't see."[7]) As is evident in this poem, one of her chief roads to humor is her way of combining the adult and the child. Certainly this three-year-old is oddly wise. Unlike the rest of us, who are "trapped in a grown-up carapace" (*CP,* 437), Stevie Smith has not forgotten what it was like to be a child. She sees, and keeps telling us, that the emperor has no clothes, a fact we long ago ceased to notice, much less to mention.

The theme of rejection takes a variety of unexpected forms, and it is chiefly this unexpectedness which constitutes the humor. Parents give their children stupid advice: "Mother said if I wore this hat/I would be certain to get off with the right sort of chap." Being a dutiful child, she does wear her hat; and the hat itself instantly runs off with her, landing her on a "peculiar island."

> Am I glad I am here? Yes, well, I am,
> It's nice to be rid of Father, Mother and the young man
> There's just one thing causes me a twinge of pain,
> If I take my hat off, shall I find myself home again?
> So in this early morning land I always wear my hat
> Go home, you see, well I wouldn't run a risk like that.
>
> ("My Hat," *CP,* 315)

7. Ibid., 40.

The implicit assumption that home is dangerous constitutes the incongruity and the humor. A more ghoulish rejection occurs in "The Wedding Photograph." This tittering girl, behatted though she is, has married to get away from home. "It is the death wish lights my beautiful eyes," she tells us. However, the term "death wish" here has a double meaning, since the speaker means by it not so much her own death as her husband's. That is what she is thinking:

> Goodbye Harry I must have you by me for a time
> But once in the jungle you must go off to a higher clime
> . . . .
> So smile Harry smile and I will smile too
> Thinking what is going to happen to you.
>
> (*CP,* 425)

In a similar jungle metaphor, Lady Singleton rejects her Henry, although she does not wish him dead — merely absent:

> I am not a cold woman, Henry,
> But I do not feel for you,
> What I feel for the elephants and miasmas
> And the general view.
>
> ("Lady 'Rogue' Singleton," *CP,* 194)

Smith's uncommitted people die rather happily, not despising those who pounce on the artifacts they are abandoning. In the picture which accompanies "The Death of Mr. Mounsel," the young lady looks healthy and even rather sexy (a rarity in Smith's drawings), while Mr. Mounsel looks quite miserable But in the poem itself he begins allusively and self-importantly: "I am dying, Egypt, dying/Keep my watch and send word home," happily mentioning that in the grave he will be "Unmolested quit of danger" (*CP,* 76), free of watches and girls together. In some of the poems, the impulse to reject becomes simply unpleasant; but this kind of failure is luckily rare.

The Wedding Photograph

The Frog Prince

Death of Mr. Mounsel

Nature and Free Animals

Sketches by Stevie Smith.

People who evade commitment also resist other kinds of change. Smith liked to draw familiar mythological characters into her own views. Dido welcomes death as the one lover who won't leave her, and Persephone relishes the "wintriness of

Hades" (*CP,* 248). "The Frog Prince," shown looking slightly inebriated in the accompanying illustration, is so used to being a frog that he is not really sure he wants to be disenchanted, although he knows that this change is inevitable, and that it will be "heavenly."

> I can be happy until you come
> But I cannot be heavenly,
> Only disenchanted people
> Can be heavenly.
>
> (*CP,* 407)

The word "heavenly" carries the rich and various mixture one finds so often in Stevie Smith's poetry. In contemporary slang it means "simply marvelous," but it also means being translated beyond death; and it reflects Smith's more usual theme that heavenliness is available after death. Meanwhile, the idea of a frog loving his frogginess is certainly an amusing shift in point of view.

Smith's view of animals is intense and original. Like Blake, she objects to their enslavement by men; but unlike Blake, she also objects to God, unable to decide whether he is "good, impotent or unkind" (*CP,* 52). In the picture appended to a poem called "Nature and Free Animals," the unfortunate man in the illustration appears to be sticking his tongue out at the monstrous animal created by God and man, uneasy at his position in a middle state.

Certainly uneasiness, melancholy, the closeness of death are always lurking near Stevie Smith's poems, no matter what the subject. The poems are unkind, even misanthropic at times, and God himself is not free from blame. Why then, is the effect so unrelentingly merry? Part of the explanation is a matter of literary technique, as in "A Soldier Dear to Us":

Oh Basil, Basil, you had such a merry heart
But you taught me a secret you did not perhaps mean to impart,

That one must speak lightly, and use fair names like the ladies
They used to call
The Eumenides.

                                                        (*CP,* 527)

Here, incidentally, we find some of the tricks Smith uses to keep
us awake and laughing — the hurried rhythms which at times
force a reader to squash a line in order to reach the rhyme in time,
and of course the occasional oddness of the rhyme, as in "ladies"
and "Eumenides." In other poems, rhymes in foreign languages
sometimes add to a feeling of arbitrariness and sheer fun reminiscent of Ogden Nash, but less glittery. As part of this process
of "speaking lightly," Smith would often shift her point of view
and tone. This shift appears in one of her simplest and most winning poems, "My Muse."

> My Muse sits forlorn
> She wishes she had not been born
> She sits in the cold
> No word she says is every told.

> Why does my Muse only speak when she is unhappy?
> She does not, I only listen when I am unhappy
> When I am happy I live and despise writing
> For my Muse this cannot but be dispiriting.

                                                        (*CP,* 405)

The girl who accompanies this poem looks both rejecting and
rejected. She sits at the lower corner of the page, hunched over,
neck gawkily leaning forward, something close to a dunce's hat
on her head. She looks adolescent, or younger, and friendless.
Everyone who writes has at one time or another jilted his muse,
and Stevie Smith has made this sad fact simple, charming, ap-
pealing.

    These poems of sadness and desperation, this strange mixture
of child and adult, of laughter and tears, does not allow us any
emotion unmingled. "Being comical," Smith says in a poem

My Muse

Was He Married?

Not Waving but Drowning

Sketches by Stevie Smith.

about Christ, "does not ameliorate the desperation." Human beings, unlike Christ, are "mixed," and their suffering is certainly greater than a god's. Gods don't have to commit themselves—they need not marry, they never sin, they are invariably adequate. In this poem, a child is asking questions about Christ, beginning with, "Was he married?" and his mother is attempting to answer, yet in the accompanying illustration, oddly, the mother is sitting at the child's knee — perhaps to point out further that human beings are "so mixed":

> All human beings should have a medal,
> A god cannot carry it, he is not able.
>
> A god is Man's doll, you ass,
> He makes him up like this on purpose.
>
> He might have made him up worse.
>
> He often has, in the past.
>
> To choose a god of love, as he did and does,
> Is a little move then?
>
> Yes, it is.
>
> A larger one will be when men
> Love love and hate hate but do not deify them?
>
> It will be a larger one.
>
> (*CP,* 389–91)

This is a hopeful poem, leading to a larger world, a better world and — note — a godless world, but Stevie Smith rarely holds out this sort of hope. She more frequently depicts the comic poignancy of the here and now. This comic poignancy is the message of what is probably her best-known poem, "Not Waving but Drowning."

> Nobody heard him, the dead man,
> But still he lay moaning:
> I was much further out than you thought
> And no waving but drowning.

Poor chap, he always loved larking
And now he's dead
It must have been too cold for him his heart gave way,
They said.

Oh, no no no, it was too cold always
(Still the dead one lay moaning)
I was much too far out all my life
And not waving but drowning.

(CP, 303)

This is the cry of a child, but of a child who has lived long
enough to look like an adult. Most adults learn to stay near shore,
but this male speaker was "much too far out all my life." He is
dead, yet he still speaks. He pities himself, yet everyone else
thought "he always loved larking"; they never saw through the
external merriment into the sadness. Stevie Smith at times reveled in her melancholy, vied to be sadder than anyone else. "If
you attempt to be more melancholy than me I shall be more than
furious: I shall be *hurt*. I felt too low for words (eh?) last weekend, but worked it off for all that in a poem, and *Punch* like it,
think it *funny* I suppose. It was touching, I thought — called
'Not Waving but Drowning.'"[8] Although she twitted *Punch* for
finding the poem funny, her own illustration is decidedly incongruous. The speaker is a man, but here we have a girl surely
standing only waist deep, neither waving nor drowning, simply
peering through wet hair. Stevie Smith said she chose her illustrations arbitrarily, but seeming capriciousness is a technique in
her poetry, and simply because an illustration seems incongruous
is no reason to dismiss it. The illustration in this case can only
pique the reader's amusement. By adding this picture, Smith
further intermingled all the experiences we are so busily dock-
eting, and trounced our fears of death and other inevitabilities.
Later, even at that moment when her brain tumor had weakened
her beyond repair, she could laugh at her own extinction; note

8. Ibid., 59.

one final time the fact that Death is the only God who is dutiful, and demote him to a lowercase *g*: "Ah me, sweet Death, you are the only god/Who comes as a servant when he is called." Her danse macabre is always so vital, death and life seem to be so inextricably mixed, that we leave her feeling braver, able to laugh at whatever comes our way.

1978

*

Play, Fantasy, and Strange Laughter
Stevie Smith's Uncomfortable Poetry

MARTIN PUMPHREY

> Miss Pauncefort sang at the top of her voice
> (Sing tirry-lirry-lirry down the lane)
> And nobody knew what she sang about
> (Sing tirry-lirry-lirry all the same)[1]

Stevie Smith's off-key, enigmatically childish poetry has always irritated as much as charmed her critics. It fits no obvious category and, though Smith's popularity as a novelist as well as a poet has continued to grow since her death in 1971, her critical reputation remains ambiguous and unconfirmed. Superficially, her poems seem as familiar and easily accessible as the snippets of English life and the nursery jingles out of which they are constructed. At the same time, taken together, they constitute a stubbornly self-contained body of work that shows few signs of involvement in "the gang warfare" that preoccupied British and American writers immediately before and after World War II. Mocking but not committed, arch rather than revolutionary, neither distinctly "romantic" nor "classicist," Smith stands out as a willful, isolated, slightly worrying figure, someone much easier to humor and patronize than engage in debate. Disturbed

1. Stevie Smith, *The Collected Poems of Stevie Smith* (London: Allen Lane, 1975), 30.

by her poetry's obvious, even perverse refusal to be "literary," her critics have often shown exasperation. They have applauded the *faux naïf* style but been more at ease all too clearly with the poems that "look down deep into the soul of suffering humanity"[2] or "display the strong and sternly pure rhetoric" that reminds them (one senses the relief) of Lawrence or Blake.[3] Philip Larkin regretted her "facetious bosh" and, with judicious, coercive friendliness, the majority of her critics have agreed "her frivolity devalues her seriousness." Those few who have committed time to her work have either isolated individual poems for New Critical inspection or (of a more Romantic persuasion) probed for the authentic presence behind the masks and voices to validate their sense that Smith is an interesting (if minor) writer. Most of this has been misguided, not only because it seems to stem from an unacknowledged desire to defend the literary categories the poetry so obviously contests but, more crucially, because it reflects an attempt to pass Smith off as respectable. Such an approach must inevitably be self-defeating. Any discussion of Smith's poetry that is to do more than confirm it as an amusingly idiosyncratic, critical anomaly must confront the implications of the uncompromising use of play and fantasy that is its most distinctive characteristic. To single out as important simply those poems that can be read most easily as "serious literature" is to evade the critical challenge of Smith's full poetic performance.

The particular construction of "seriousness" that has traditionally validated the procedures of English Literary Studies is at issue here. Like "excessive" popularity, ephemerality, and idiosyncrasy, play and fantasy have been construed as negative categories against which the literary canon is defined. Though historically the canon may have changed, the deployment of those categories has consistently directed "serious" (mainstream) literary debate and justified the ignoring of those traditions now

2. "On a Broomstick," *Times Literary Supplement,* 1 Dec. 1950, 771.
3. Philip Larkin, "Stevie, Good-bye," *Observer,* 23 Jan. 1972, 28.

constituted (often with dubious numerical accuracy) as "the literature of minorities." In relation to the critical reception of Stevie Smith's poetry, the point has particular relevance. To label a poem, or in reality a major portion of a poet's work, "facetious bosh" places it outside the pale of sympathetic debate and makes any discussion of the alternatives it explores impossible. Thus, though Smith's irony and "witch-like wisdom" have been noted (the latter mostly for some byplay about broomsticks), her critics have ignored the rather obvious question of why someone who so manifestly enjoyed playing games should refuse, throughout a long career and at the obvious risk of critical obscurity, to play *the* game. The question redirects critical attention and challenges the commonsense distinction between play and "seriousness" that Smith's critics have accepted too readily.

Play, as play theorists over the past thirty years or more have demonstrated, has a complex range of functions. Play activities (at all ages) involve the learning and recognition of cultural categories. Certainly too they can, and often do, involve the exploring and subverting of categories. Play requires the recognition that, in any act of communication, it is framing that categorizes and thus fixes the stable meanings of what are otherwise infinitely meaningful (or meaningless) gestures. The signal "This is play," as Gregory Bateson pointed out in 1955, is in fact a signal about signals, an act of metacommunication that defines the context in which a particular set of gestures is to be read. If it is to be understood, both sender and receiver must be able to recognize the paradoxical statement that (to use Bateson's terms) "the playful nip denotes the bite but . . . does not denote what would be denoted by the bite."[4] Here the "recognition" is implicit of course. With bluff and playful threat, on the other hand, the framing process is made both overt and problematic. In this case, the initiating signal is an interrogative one ("Is this play?") that faces the receiver with contradictory possible read-

4. "A Theory of Play and Fantasy," in *Steps to an Ecology of Mind* (London: Granada, 1973), 150–66.

ings of particular gestures. Like literary irony, teasing is a "pluralistic way of speaking" that tests the relationship between speaker and listener. For the uninitiated it can create misunderstanding and unresolvable problems of interpretation. For the initiated, it confirms complicity.

Smith's poetry not only draws on children's culture for its form and content but knowingly exploits the interrogative play signal to challenge conventional literary and cultural frames and unsettle the reader's assumptions about the relationship with the text. Quite evidently her teasing segregates her readers into those who opt for the simple stability of the notion that "this is play" (and therefore need not be investigated) and those who pursue the ramifications of the challenge her teasing presents. That challenge is fundamental. In terms of conventional literary framing, Smith's flippancy, carelessness, and redundancies, her refusal to commit her authority to a single voice or point of view, her childishness, use of fairy tales, nursery rhymes, and oral literature all signal that her writing is nonserious, verse not poetry, fun not Literature. Read in this way, its obvious ironies, though recognizable, are contained and defused.

If, on the other hand, the reader pursues the destabilizing effects of the question "Is this play?" then he/she is forced to consider the nature of the complicity the poems invite and to recognize the ambivalent, carnivalesque quality of their laughter that is at once challenging, self-mocking, and subversive.[5] From this perspective, it becomes evident that Smith juxtaposed the (private/secret) world of play and magical possibility with the (public) known world of the conventionally Real in order to contest cultural forms and assumptions. Under the mask of oddness and triviality, through the voices and experiences of her fantasy characters, her poems repeatedly investigate the difficulties of negotiating between inner desires and outer restraint and contemplate the allure and danger of resistance and transgression.

5. "Carnival laughter" — the reference is to Mikhail Bakhtin, *Rabelais and His World,* trans. Helene Iswolsky (Cambridge, Mass.: MIT Press, 1968).

That the private experience of the poems is constantly (not exclusively) associated with the powerlessness and trivialization known particularly to women and children cannot go unnoticed. Smith is not a writer who can be easily recruited as a feminist. The painstakingly constructed, conservative, suburban identity and her critical attitude to what she saw as simplistic and spurious attempts to identify women writers as a group make such a maneuver impossible.[6] At the same time, a reading of her poetry that takes account of her as a woman writing seems to clarify precisely those difficulties that have most taxed her critics. Approached in this way, Smith's "oddness" identifies her with other women writers whose poetic strategies have been directed not toward the construction of an authoritative and consistent poetic persona or self but toward disruption, discontinuity, and indirection. Such otherwise substantially different writers as Rossetti, Dickinson, Stein, Plath, and Rich come to mind here. Elaine Showalter has recently argued that embedded in women's writing are the distinctive patterns of women's expressive behavior, identifiable strategies of (covert) resistance to the silencing or muting experienced by women within mainstream culture. Showalter has suggested that "women's writing is a double-voiced discourse that always embodies the social, literary and cultural heritages of both the muted and the dominant." Her point is born out here; for as the reader vacillates between uncritically discarding Smith's poems as "play" (therefore frivolous and simple) or becoming involved in the implications of their teasing, he/she is forced (in Showalter's words) "to keep two alternative, oscillating texts simultaneously in view . . . (is forced to see distinct from the orthodox text) another text . . . more or less muted . . . but always there to be read."[7] If one does read the poems from this point of view, it becomes far less important to

6. See for example Stevie Smith, "The Better Half" and "Poems in Petticoats," in *Me Again: Uncollected Writings of Stevie Smith*, ed. Jack Barbera and William McBrien (London: Virago Press, 1981).

7. "Feminist Criticism in the Wilderness," *Critical Inquiry* (Winter 1981): 179–205.

try to identify a single, consistent voice (a Stevie Smith) in the poems than to note that the multiple voices of Smith's children, women, and fantasy characters often speak through and are seldom fully at ease with the languages and conventions that make up the discourses of their cultural (and the author's literary) environment. The perception identifies not only the consistent direction of Smith's everpresent irony but the coherence of her poetry *as a whole.* It is the poetic performance not individual poems that must be considered. Smith's voices speak from muted areas that lie behind/beyond and are radically detached from the surface of mainstream culture. Through indirection, inversion, paradox, and riddle, they focus attention on the assumptions embedded in the fabric of communication itself.

The extensive use Smith made of children's expressive forms (of nursery rhymes and fairy tales in particular) is immediately obvious of course. Since her critics' attention has been directed elsewhere, however, the range and authority of her references and the subtlety with which she integrated the elements she selected has been ignored. Her use of nursery rhymes — their subject matter, narratives, and characters, their imaginative license and irregular metrical structures — nicely illustrates the point. In formal terms, for example, one can identify without difficulty her use of counting rhymes ("Tenuous and Precarious"), toe rhymes ("Nipping Pussy's Feet in Fun"), jingles ("Hippy-Mo"), dandling rhymes ("My Cats"), lullabies ("Farewell"), skipping rhymes ("Mr. Over" and "Proffitt and Batten"), riddles ("The Ambassador"), word games ("The Celtic Fringe" and "Her-zie") as well as specific references to Lewis Carroll ("The Passing Cloud"), and more general references to the tradition of "nonsense verse."[8] Occasionally the formal structure of a nursery rhyme is maintained throughout a whole poem (the counting rhyme of "Tenuous and Precarious" for example). More usually however the specific reference is no more than a residual trace, an

8. These are categories used by Iona Opie and Peter Opie in *The Oxford Nursery Rhyme Book* (Oxford: Oxford Univ. Press, 1955).

opening phrase or an ambiguously repeated refrain that sets in motion the clash of form and content that creates the poetry's characteristically enigmatic voice and tone.

In thematic terms, the poems consistently integrate nursery rhyme elements to exploit the contradictory possibilities in the cultural construction of the child (as innocent/depraved, conservative/anarchist, naïve/gifted-with-insight) and thus challenge the reader to distinguish between the triviality and truthfulness of the child's-eye perspective. More broadly, the imaginative license of the nursery rhyme makes possible the division in Smith's poetry between the stable authoritarian, restrictive world of adults and the linked, fluid worlds of play and fairy land that are inhabited by children, animals, supernatural characters, women, poets, and the muse. Emphasized by Smith's nursery book drawings, this division affects the reading of poems in which it is not itself obviously evident. Thus, whether it is the genteel world of the English upper-middle class, the bourgeois world of suburbia, the world of offices or domestic drudgery, the adult world of the poems is dull, mechanical, a place of forms without meaning. There children are sentimentalized and trivialized; women are enshrined and enslaved. Both groups are powerless; both are silenced. Significantly, though male power is seldom displayed or even visible it is ever present. Rooted in the forms and assumptions of cultural constructions, coercion is subtle, friendly, civilized. It is mothers, aunts, and governesses, not fathers, who try to convince their daughters to accept that "marred pleasures are best," take up "the headache and the crown" and follow the path of female duty (*CP,* 313).

Subversion is never far away. The nursery only ambiguously affirms the control of the adult world. A place of banishment and restraint, it is also a place for innovation and rebellion. Repeatedly the poems ridicule the assumptions of adults and the insidious socializing intent with which they intrude into children's lives. Institutional games (as opposed to play) and the fairy tales and nursery rhymes co-opted by adults for didactic purposes provide the contexts for resistance. Sometimes the point is made directly by a rebellious adult like the woman spoilsport who urges girls to resist "the balsy nonsense" of the games ethic ("I will let down the side if I get a chance/And I will sell the pass for a couple of pence," *CP*, 167). Elsewhere the anarchic force of children's culture simply ignores control. There are the children, for example, who resist the advice of "the awful aging couple" by letting it "in at one ear and out at the other" (*CP*, 174); or there is the girl who is willing to be silenced so that by keeping her thoughts to herself they will in the end "shine as a white worm shines under a green boulder" (*CP*, 204). With word games, nonsense, and "silliness" Smith's children evade the entrapments of language. Of "Duty Is My Lobster" Smith herself commented: "This poem turns on duty. You see the child has been told that duty is one's lodestar. But she is rebellious, this child, she will have none of it, so she says lobster instead of lodestar, and so makes a mock of it, and makes a monkey of the kind teacher" (*Me Again*, 111).

The possibility of contradictory readings that Smith's apparently simple use of nursery rhymes and children's play can create is well illustrated in "Tender Only to One," the title poem of her second collection of poems published in 1938. The girl's game involving the plucking of petals from a flower to decide "a lover" is a familiar one; here its repetitions create the structure for a speaker's contemplation of her social world and final assertion of independence.

> Tender only to one
> Tender and true
> The petals swing
> To my fingering
> Is it you, or you, or you?
>
> Tender only to one
> I do not know his name
> And the friends who fall
> To the petals' call
> May think my love to blame.

Tender only to one
This petal holds a clue
The face it shows
But too well knows
Who I am tender to.

Tender only to one,
Last petal's breath
Cries out aloud
From the icy shroud
His name, his name is Death

(*CP,* 93)

On the surface this seems trite, a jingle without significance. Its playfulness, however, suggests, I think, at least three distinctly contradictory readings. The game "teaches" the virtue of female purity and absolute faithfulness. A game of chance, it also implies the passivity a young girl must learn in relation to the events that will touch her life most closely. It is the ideal embodied in the traditional fairy-tale princess and, at first glance, it might seem to be affirmed by the poem. Quite clearly, however, the melodramatic posturing of the last line ("His name, his name is Death") suggests something different. Read ironically, the last verse signals not a happy acceptance of the nunlike purity that willingly embraces the spiritual release of death but a recognition of the exclusions and denial of desire the ideal demands. Reread in this way, the poem suggests both the futility of the ideal that logically can only be realized in the frozen stasis of death and the isolation in life that will result if the speaker abandons "the friends who fall to the petals' call." Worse, in so far as she does faithfully isolate herself, she must bear the guilt created by the conflicting demands of the chosen ONE and the rejected many "who will think her love to blame."

These two contradictory readings reflect the confusion that develops about the identity, age, and knowingness of the speaker. It is a confusion caused by the ambiguity of the framing signal. If the poem begins with a playfulness signaled by the echo of the child's game, it ends with an enigmatic and challenging inconclusiveness. Is this play or not-play? The perception of Death as the gentleman caller suggests an adult, literary seriousness. The speaker's opening pose, on the other hand, is that of the child who knows her play is being observed and whose gestures and words as a result are in part private and in part directed at an audience that will be both invited into and excluded from the game. This teasing introduces a third possibility. Under its cover ("I'm playing alone but I know you're listening and do/don't want you to hear") the speaker mocks the literary expectation that she will give herself to her reader. Archly holding herself back ("Is it you, or you, or you?") she commits herself to nobody. Just as the girl in "White Thought" subversively agrees to be silenced, so here the speaker elusively manipulates the mask of female reserve. Coyly playing off a possible physical lover against a spiritual lover, Death, and both against the reader, she turns the mask into a weapon with which to achieve freedom from the demands of being "tender only to one." As the different readings within the text emerge, their contradictory possibilities challenge the reader not only to consider the coercion inherent in the girl's game but also the power that can be achieved by the playful manipulation of the feminine mask. Though the poem may appear trite, its teasing sets in motion the destabilizing ambiguity that will play over the poems it introduces.

Smith used fairy tales to confirm her identification with the nursery and children's culture. She used them also to explore the existential ramifications of cultural resistance. The interest is clear in her earliest work but (as she did the classical myths) she came to exploit the tales with increasing regularity. Sometimes a named tale creates the structure for a whole poem)"The Frog Prince" for example). More often a recognizable source provides only a starting point, title, single line, or significant reference (as in "Rapunzel, Rapunzel"). Most usually the fairy-tale elements (characters, events, symbols) are unspecific in origin and serve simply to establish the possibilities of fairy magic as an alternative to the reductive logic of conventional common sense. Where the popular children's selections produced by the nineteenth-century vogue for fairy tales emphasized the socially acceptable happy ending and the gender stereotypes of the passive princess and the active prince, Smith returned to the Grimm brothers' tales to rediscover, beneath the editings and reeditings, the cruel, destructive laughter of Eulenspieglei, the trickster. Behind the mirror or the closed door, beneath the water's surface, in the wild wood lies an enchanted world of inexhaustible possibilities from which the muse and the subversive voices of the poems can be heard calling, and into which the characters of the poems stray to be awakened and transformed. Significantly, since it reverses the emphasis of the popular anthologies, Smith's attention is usually focused on the activities and choices of the women and girls who experience the fairy world and learn "to speak contrariwise." Significantly too, since that magic world is consistently associated with self-discovery, transgression, and art, the freedom it offers is ambiguous. Though alluring, it is also frightening and dangerous.

Certainly the alternative truths that fairy magic reveals are not "pretty" any more than the harsh laughter of the trickster or the howling of the liberated muse. Their effects are often painful and dislocating. Ruthlessly, without warning, they cut through the euphemisms and hypocrisies of genteel society to shatter conventional assumptions. In "Silence and Tears" for example, the sudden intervention of the bird ("Pee-wee sang the little bird upon the tree again and again," *CP,* 110) seems at first inexplicable. On its surface the poem, rather blandly, ridicules the hypocrisy of a family of mourners and the vanity of the clergy. The bird's voice, however, suggests a more ugly reality. It speaks from perhaps the most macabre of the Grimms' tales, "The Juniper Tree," part of which the brothers, in their original rendering, said they felt it "right to omit,"[9] There it carries the other-

9. *Grimms' Fairy Tales,* trans. Edgar Taylor (London: Scolar Press, 1979), 2:254.

wise hidden story of a child butchered by his stepmother and eaten by his father. Here, without warning, its intervention (emphasized by Smith's own line drawing) expands the poem's light satire to imply a grotesque comment on the abuse of family power concealed beneath civilized appearances.

Whether it is an advantage to see so much and so deeply is left open to question. "Would people be so sympathetic if they knew how the story went," the speaker asks only to conclude, "best not put it to the test. Silence and tears are convenient." Taken together the poems are ambiguous on this point. While they challenge and invert the symbolic order the fairy tales have been traditionally co-opted to affirm—by ridiculing the expectations of the prince or asserting the rebellious independence of the princess — they show quite clearly that the experience of fairyland can, in its turn, isolate and make strange. "Now I'm home," laments one character who has returned to the normal world, "there's nobody I know" (*CP,* 487). Worse still, as in traditional tales, the magical transformations of fairyland can be frighteningly irreversible. The point is worth examination for it suggests the complexity that lies behind Smith's poetic performance.

In "The Lady from the Well Spring," the little girl, Joan, makes a journey to an enchanted world (overtly linked with art by the subtitle reference to Renoir's *La Source*), finds she prefers it to the social world she has left, and chooses not to return. The civilized drawing room, dominated by the sophistication of "the French Ladies" with which the poem opens, is presented in images of masks and imprisonment ("As the French Ladies laughed their white faces/barred by the balcony shadows seemed to grimace"). Excluded from their genteel gossip, Joan none the less hears the ladies talking of someone ("he") who needs rescuing from "the Lady of the Well Spring" and, with subtle naïveté, makes their comments an excuse for her own escape. Passing quickly, in a fairy-tale transition, from the drawing room to the wild wood, Joan encounters cacophonous sounds and lush vegetation.

Into a little wood
She runs, the branches catching at her feet draw blood
And there is a sound of piping screaming croaking clacking
And now as she runs there is a bicker
Of a stream growing narrower in a trickle
And a splash and a flinging, it is water springing.

(*CP,* 311)

In the luxuriance of this world, she meets the Lady of the well spring, "a fair smooth lady whose stomach swelling full breast fine waist and long legs tapering are shadowed with grass-green streaks." As the parallels between the iron bar shadows of the one and the grass green shadows of the other suggest, both the world of civilized sophistication and the anarchic, fertile wood are potential prisons. Forced to choose, Joan opts for the wild.

The wood is manifestly a place of female power. Indeed, if one follows Ellen Moer's argument in *Literary Women* (chap. 11), it is quite clearly constructed as "a female landscape." The lady's fatness (the specific choice of words is surely significant) suggests not the voluptuous appeal to the male eye found in Renoir's paintings but a self-oriented sensuality that contrasts directly with the publicly confirmed "freedom" of the sophisticated society women. Again, however, ambiguities creep in. Though the speaker's voice supports Joan's choice ("Do not think of her as one who looses" the poem concludes), the luxuriance of the magic wood barely conceals its menace. Its voices are harsh; its plants wound. The fairy world, at best, offers an imperfect alternative. For Joan, here, or Persephone in Smith's inversion of the classical myth (*CP,* 248) or the changeling child who goes off into the storm in "Eulenspieglei" (*CP,* 98) that alternative is clearly preferable to the everyday world they know. For them fairy captivity is freedom. For others however it is far less pleasurable. The northern lake to which the "small lady" (*CP,* 471) is transported by an idle wish is a cold, dark empty space, devoid of human society. Though Persephone can conclude, when she has chosen the underworld, "in this wintriness is my happiness," the women of the poems face an impossible choice. While marriage, domesticity, and the ideal of Purity in terms of which female desire is culturally constructed may silence, subordinate, and isolate women, at the same time, they offer the security and protection of a known world. To accept them promises social recognition. To resist and transgress risks isolation and hardship. "If I say 'I'm valuable' . . . I shall be alone" protests one young girl (*CP,* 448) when urged to think more of herself, and her protest neatly pinpoints the equally strong lure of resistance and acceptance that Smith's archly crafted, powerfully ambiguous poetic performance strives to negotiate.

I began with the argument that a perception of the carnivalesque possibilities of play and fantasy makes possible a reading of those areas of Smith's poetry her critics have otherwise dismissed as "facetious bosh." The consistent presence of play and fantasy elements in her poetry, I have suggested, provides both the means and the cover for cultural and social subversion. It also fundamentally challenges the concept of "seriousness" that validates the discourses that make up the mainstream of English studies. Since they have been slow to acknowledge the nature of that challenge, Smith's critics have had little reason to examine the implications of the way in which it is expressed. Why, it seems obvious to ask, should the poetry so studiously encourage the reader to treat it dismissively? Why, despite its constant gesturing toward the hidden and secret areas of experience, should it so resolutely evade direct personal statement and authorial commitment? The questions lead to a consideration of what Smith's teasing play implies about the relationship between private experience and public utterance, about self-presentation.

Many of Smith's poems implicitly, some identifiably, emerge from the occasions of her daily life at Palmers Green, from her work at George Newnes's publishing office off the Strand, from her reading and reviewing, from conversations, friendships, and weekend visits. Repeatedly they hint at secret and repressed desires and suggest unambiguously that play and fantasy give access to those private areas from which, however indecipherably, the voices of the muse and the inner self call. Though this may appear to suggest she shares many of their concerns, Smith cannot in any meaningful sense be grouped among the "confessional poets" of the 1950s and 1960s. Rather, to use a term that Terence Diggory coined in a discussion of Emily Dickinson, her work is "anticonfessional."[10] A comparison with her near contemporary, Robert Lowell, whose *Life Studies* of 1959 became the focus for so much critical debate about confessional poetry, provides a useful contrast. Lowell's statement that he wanted to make his reader "believe that he was getting the real Robert Lowell"[11] contains precisely those assumptions about language that Smith went out of her way to reject. Rooted in Romanticism (like the idea of organic form it co-opted), confessional poetry suggests, however hypothetically, the possibility of a fit between language and experience, the possibility of an achieved autobiographical self that will resolve the disjunction between public and private, face and mask. Smith's poetry offers no such hope. For Smith's speakers and characters, language is an alien even hostile medium. What it is that the voices of the wild wood "pipe scream croak and clack" can be expressed only indirectly through the openings broken in the surface of language by the contradictions and paradoxes created by her playful performance. In fact, when in "Look!" one of her speakers, after much labor, does retrieve in the magical, transparent fish (that comes "not from the sea-bed but from the generations," *CP,* 369) an archetypal symbol of the unknown, the poem concludes dismissively that anyway there is no one to show it to.

The "voice" so many readers hear in Smith's poetry is not in this sense equatable with a constructed, fixed identity — the poet, an achieved autobiographical self, a unified "I." Rather the

10. "Armored Women, Naked Men: Dickinson, Whitman, and Their Successors," in *Shakespeare's Sisters,* ed. Sandra M. Gilbert and Susan Gubar (Bloomington: Indiana Univ. Press, 1979), 142.

11. "Interview with Robert Lowell," *Paris Review* (Spring 1961):70.

speakers and points of view that emerge from the collected poems create a conversation, a carnivalesque performance that playfully investigates the nature and possibilities of masks. That the poems I have discussed singly contain contradictory readings and read collectively seem to veer from one stance to another, now urging resistance, now pointing to its negative consequence, now reveling in rebellion now appearing to urge acceptance, establishes the interrogative quality that is their essential characteristic. Smith permits no illusion that the formations of culture and language are anything other than constructions. Her interest is in the multiple ways in which those constructions can be used. Sometimes supportive, usually coercive, they are inescapable. Power lies, her poems suggest, not in the Romantic illusion of the created self but in the constant manipulation of the culturally defined masks by which the self is known—to create a private space behind the surface of public experience. The elusive "self" of the poems is not to be found in any one mask or image but rather, obliquely implied, in the endless play of construction and deconstruction the poems demonstrate.

In her excellent introduction to the Faber anthology of Smith's selected writing, Hermione Lee identifies the range and complexity of Smith's use of literary tradition (her links with Blake, Tennyson, Browning, Carlyle, Dickinson, Arnold, and others) and rejects the image of Smith as "the dotty spinster of Palmers Green."[12] This is certainly a necessary and long-overdue corrective. My aim, however, has been to stress the danger of trying to make Smith acceptable by comparing her with those, almost exclusively male, members of the "serious" literary canon. Smith's importance is of a very different kind. Like Emily Dickinson, who is awkwardly mismatched in that list, Smith as a poet never strives for the authoritative unity and consistency of voice that distinguishes "the great writer." She never strives, that is, for the consensus of the reviewer who singled out for praise those of her poems that "look down deep into the soul of suffering human-

12. *Stevie Smith: A Selection* (London: Faber, 1983).

ity." It is precisely the coercive (because universalizing) assumption about individual identity unwittingly revealed in that phrase that Smith's poetry most vigorously contests.

Seamus Heaney and others have commented on Smith's dramatic readings of her poems and clearly she wrote with oral performance in mind. Importantly too the idea of performance shaped her books. The flippancy, redundancy, childishness, nursery book illustrations, and contradictory statements all serve to frame the context in which the reader encounters individual poems and within which individual poems reverberate. To isolate a single poem and force it to stand alone—though many can and do—serves no purpose except to place it at a disadvantage. With her playing, Smith created a powerful protective environment for her poems. Just as the riddle that so many of them resemble operates rhetorically to put power in the hands of the questioner, so Smith's bluff and teasing puts the onus of adjustment on the reader. Within the charmed, upside-down world of her books, it is "seriousness" that must prove itself, the "Real" that must justify its claim to authority.[13]

1986

13. My thanks here to Gill Alexander and David Richards for pointers and suggestions.

⁜

Stevie, Good-bye

PHILIP LARKIN

Two of my favorite quotations are "The business of a poet is to move the reader's heart by showing his own" and "Only mediocrities develop." Both applied to Stevie Smith's poems, and this posthumous collection [*Scorpion and Other Poems*] shows it was so to the end.

Poetry today being what it is, she had long ceased to seem eccentric or freakish. Her method was to take a potshot at anything that, poetically, took her fancy, and the subjects she held up triumphantly forced us time and time again to admit there had been something there after all. They are an extraordinary collection: cats, Excalibur, childhood, Racine, Cranmer, Fafnir, and the Occasional Yarrow are jumbled with strange refinements of feeling and situation — almost, as in "Autumn," capsule novels: —

> He told his life story to Mrs. Courtly
> Who was a widow. "Let us get married shortly,"
> He said. "I am no longer passionate,
> But we can have some conversation before it is too late."

She showed her heart by blurting things out, artlessly, in a *faux-naif* style, as in "Voices against England in the Night," that enabled her to slide from Daisy Ashford/Lorelei Lee mannerisms at one end of the scale to a strong and sternly pure rhetoric at the other, a reminiscence of Lawrence and Blake: —

114

But they cried: Could not England, once the world's best,
Put off her governing garment and be better dressed
In a shroud, a shroud? O history turn thy pages fast!

Did she move her readers? On occasion, certainly: a handful of
poems—"Not Waving but Drowning," "The Singing Cat," and
"I Remember" are three—will draw away from the rest as her
reputation settles down. Many others start well and then peter
out (in this, at any rate, she resembles Emily Dickinson, to
whom the introduction compares her, not altogether convincingly). A more serious drawback was her quaintness, frivolity,
fantasy, call it what you will: all too often one found oneself rejecting poems ("Nourish Me on an Egg, Nanny") as facetious
bosh. And sometimes the sense of bosh seeped into other poems,
so that one could never forget when reading one that this was a
Stevie Smith poem. Worse, it tended to devalue her seriousness:
for some readers, she was simply not to be taken seriously at all.

They are the losers. She was for all this a writer of individuality and integrity, who had perfected a way of writing that could
deal with any subject, and a tone of voice that could not be cop-
ied. Did she, truly, not develop? Unless one has all the books,
it's hard to be specific (a *Collected Poems* as soon as possible,
please): in her later poems she became a little sadder and more
ominous, and if this is development then to this extent she developed. But there was little or no change in style: *Scorpion* re-
news her engagement with several familiar subjects: cats ("Oh I
am a cat that likes to/Gallop about doing good"), love ("Francesca in Winter") and general reflections on the human condition
("The Word"); there is a story ("Angel Boley") that might have
been written by T. F. Powys, and another ("The House of Over-
Dew") that has little point. Her long poem "How Do You See?,"
commissioned by the *Guardian* on "a subject suitable for Whitsun," as it was put to her, deals with the Holy Spirit, and has one
of her firmest endings:—

I do not think we shall be able to bear much longer the
    dishonesty

Of clinging for comfort to beliefs we do not believe in,
For comfort, and to be comfortably free of the fear
Of diminishing good, as if truth were a convenience.
I think if we do not learn quickly, and learn to teach children,
To be good without enchantment, without the help
Of beautiful painted fairy stories pretending to be true,
Then I think it will be too much for us, the dishonesty,
And, armed as we are now, we shall kill everybody,
It will be too much for us, we shall kill everybody.

"I aspire to be broken up," she ends another poem, a note sounded, not surprisingly, throughout this last collection. "Scorpion so wishes to be gone," ends a third. "Farewell" is, inexplicably, reprinted from "Not Waving but Drowning," but "Oblivion" gathers this subject up again and expresses it a little disconsolately but with a moving conviction. In the end, though, it is "Grave by a Holm-oak" that one would pick as a valediction from this honest and arresting talent, if only because it is a better embodiment of her wintry cadences: —

You lie there, Anna,
In your grave now,
Under a snow-sky,
You lie there now.

Where have the dead gone?
Where do they live now?
Not in the grave, they say,
Then where now?

Tell me, tell me,
Is it where I may go?
Ask not, says the holm-oak,
Weep, says snow.

1972

The Writer

Assessing the genius of Stevie Smith has not been easy. Such an assessment has challenged a barrage of critics and writers all of whom have found Stevie's art fascinating but somehow elusive. They collectively pay tribute to her multifaceted talent by the variety of their interpretations and evaluations. In the end Stevie's simplicity disarms all, and her profundity remains metronomically a moving target.

The poet D. J. Enright finds the Greek connection in Stevie's work: austerity, simplicity, stoicism — the classical virtues. Her anarchy is refreshing in this age of conformity.

Michael Tatham argues that Stevie Smith is one of the very few major religious poets of our time. As we live in an age without faith, it is comforting to find a poet searching her own doubt as we do ours.

Michael Horovitz, a close friend of Stevie, delights in showing how the poet used wit, intelligence, and circumstance as grist for her creative mill. He sees her struggling to reconcile the apparent disunity of life with her great desire for harmonization.

Stephen Wade indicates that Stevie wants myth, for her one of the great overawing life forces, to be considered, like religion, a major unit of personal significance. She shows that myth can be treated in ways other than intellectually.

Mark Storey suggests that the uniqueness of Stevie's art may be found in the way her work comes to terms with death. The mutual respect between scrupulous poet and discerning reader bodes well for Stevie's growing reputation and her place in the canon of twentieth-century British poetry.

Christopher Ricks compares Stevie Smith to Samuel Beckett in her use of profound fooling and the comic absurd. Her seemingly simple work disguises a sapient innocence and a studied naturalness.

The poet Seamus Heaney notes that Stevie's concerns are central to a compassionate writer: death, waste, loneliness, cruelty, the maimed, the stupid, the innocent, and the trusting. Her poetry is as archetypal as the fairy tale, the nursery song, and the folk ballad.

The final word on Stevie Smith has not been written, not by a long shot, for Stevie continues to speak to the wise child in all of us, expressing our bewilderment over the complexities of modern urban life, our fear of great and impersonal power, and our terror of the unknown, which waits in life and after.

*

Did Nobody Teach You?

D. J. ENRIGHT

The vivacious narrator of *Novel on Yellow Paper,* who claims to have written a long poem entitled "La Fille de Minos et de Pasiphaë," declares a constitutional preference for Racine over Shakespeare. A French preference, obviously, and the reasons she gives are French (the admirer of Shakespeare will present much the same account as grounds for his admiration): Shakespeare's verse is "conventional" whereas the feeling is "so warm and so human and so disturbing," and for Pompey Casmilus this is an antithesis which makes her feel "distraught and ill at ease." Then there are too many complications in Shakespeare's plots, too many inessentials, too many (if beautiful) distractions. "The plot of a tragedy must be bone-straight and simple." Pompey has strong opinions about a number of serious matters, and distinct feelings (she is not unfeeling at all!), but she does not like a riot of emotion: "I do not like it at all." Thus she is at home with *Phèdre* because "Racine is very serene, very severe, very austere and simple . . . And this tragedy is also very bracing . . . very strong and very inevitable and impersonal."

These adjectives, or some of them, could be applied to Stevie Smith's own poetry. Severe, austere, simple, bracing, impersonal. If "this is truly Greek, and what the Greek is," then Stevie Smith is somewhat Greek. If to be classical is not to be romantic (in a number of senses of that peculiar adjective), then she is in some senses classical. Like these adjectives, she is equivocal, not

119

half as simple as she seems. For instance, there is a sparsity of great expectations in her outlook, or so it would appear. The Frog Prince is "fairly happy in a frog's doom":

> I have been a frog now
> For a hundred years
> And in all this time
> I have not shed many tears . . .

Why change? To have the *heavenly* time which the story promises once the princess has kissed him, he must free himself from his contentment, for perhaps it is part of the spell "to make much of being a frog," and open himself to disenchantment:

> Come, then, royal girl and royal times,
> Come quickly,
> I can be happy until you come
> But I cannot be heavenly,
> Only disenchanted people
> Can be heavenly.

The poem is not simple and straightforward, after all, because of that ambiguous word *heavenly,* which is both flapper-talk and terribly eschatological (or something else very serious), and here, it seems, modulates from one sense into the other, so that finally it is the "romance" of living under a spell, in a frog's paradise as it were, that is to be exposed, not the romance which the fairy story holds out as the palace-living princess-loving future. Finally, to stand a chance of being "heavenly," you must be a man, undeluded.

If in the upshot this poem doesn't have much to say one way or the other about great expectations, it is an apt illustration of something else: that (as no doubt in Racine and in the Greeks) "bone-straight and simple" doesn't necessarily mean shallow or obvious, and while you can usually dart through Miss Smith's poems with immediate enjoyment, some of them are deep and (though they make no overt demand in this direction) deserve

and repay considerable thought. Among such substantial pieces
are "I Had a Dream . . . ," "The Last Turn of the Screw," "The
Airy Christ," "Come On, Come Back," and "The Crown of
Gold."

If classicism is avoidance of the romantic, then one can adduce
her best-known because most obvious attributes: the perverse
off-rhyming (she goes out of her way to rhyme impurely, but at
other times thumps down on the most obvious if pure rhyme),
the inevitably comic and deflatory effect of rhyming English
words with French, and the bathos which W. McGonagall
achieved effortlessly but she had to work for. Thus "Saffron" concludes on an inept rhyme, which reins in the reader abruptly, *and*
with an austerely negative way-of-putting-it:

> Bice, Pale and Saffron but I love best
> Beautiful summer Saffron, running fast.
> Because this beautiful spirit should not be frozen
> And is furthest from it when she is saffron.

Lest "Hymn to the Seal," in its celebration of "God's creatures
in their prime," should wax too grandiose, the middle stanza
runs thus:

> When thou wast young thy coat
> Was pale with spots upon it,
> But now in single black it lies
> And thou, Seal, liest on it.

"The Small Lady" with her large washing machine, victim of a
malicious witch, is shown as remonstrating in this way:

> "Aroint thee, false witch!" cried the lady with a brave face,
> "Human inventions help properly, magic is a disgrace."

A good sentiment, surely, but somewhat reductively expressed.
The philosophical dialogue between Eve and the Virgin Mary is

left to continue, but the report on the proceedings terminates on a strong note of definitive inconclusiveness:

> And they talked until nightfall,
> But the difference between them was radical.

And in what is surely a very serious poem, "A Man I Am," with the reminiscence of Blake often remarked on in her work and a rather more pronounced flavor of the seventeenth century (particularly Herbert and Vaughan), the resonant lines

> But presently the spring broke in
> Upon the pastures of my sin

are followed by the deliberately flat

> My poor heart bled like anything,

and in turn this is succeeded by

> And falling ill, I soon grew worse.
> Until at last I cried on Him,
> Before whom angel faces dim,
> To take the burden of my sin
> And break my head beneath his wing.

Stevie Smith's Christianity—she described herself as an agnostic Anglican, and she seems to me to have known a lot about Christianity, what it was, or what it could be—was no phantom spiritual state, no theological preserve or Sunday subject, but very much part and parcel of everyday life. Perhaps the sensed kinship with George Herbert resides here.

"Unromantic" too are her reservations on the subject of love. Or love as it is generally written about. "Anger's Freeing Power" tells of a raven who fancies himself a captive in a cell which has

only three walls. The loving narrator cannot persuade the bird
that in fact he is free to fly away, but then two other ravens come
along and jeer at him in a nicely vulgar manner:

> You wretched bird, conceited lump
> You well deserve to pine and thump.

This treatment works wonders: "Oh do I then? he says," and off
he flies to heaven's skies. The narrator is left to muse ruefully:

> Yet when I woke my eyes were wet
> To think Love had not freed my pet
>
> Anger it was that won him hence
> As only Anger taught him sense
>
> Often my tears fall in a shower
> Because of Anger's freeing power.

Here she is close to Blake, that unromantic romantic and angel-
seeing realist: "Damn braces. Bless relaxes," and "The tygers of
wrath are wiser than the horses of instruction." Her Christ, too,
is more tiger than lamb—"He is Noble, he is not Mild."

While part of her is in sympathy with dreamers, for to dream
is human, part of her remains cool, sceptical, and admonitory,
and sometimes with an effect of what Derwent May has called
"comic, forthright, moral knockabout," as in "Be Off!":

> I'm sorry to say my dear wife is a dreamer,
> And as she dreams she gets paler and leaner.
> "Then be off to your Dream, with his fly-away hat,
> I'll stay with the girls who are happy and fat."

"Accidie poisons the soul stream," as Pompey reminds us. Life
has to go on, despite dreams and dreamers; and if the dreamer
can be shaken into sense, then he or she should be. We observe
how the poet passes with relief from "Dear Female Heart":

> Dear Female Heart, I am sorry for you,
> You must suffer, that is all that you can do.
> But if you like, in common with the rest of the human race,
> You may also look most absurd with a miserable face —

to "Alfred the Great":

> Honour and magnify this man of men
> Who keeps a wife and seven children on £2 10
> Paid weekly in an envelope
> And yet he never has abandoned hope.

Miss Smith could be grim. The woman chatting harmlessly on the omnibus in "Northumberland House," it transpires, is on her way to a lunatic asylum: the poet characteristically employs the old noneuphemism. And the gentleman uttering pious sentiments over a grave —

> Farewell for ever, well for ever fare,
> The soul whose body lies beneath this stone! —

is revealed as the murderer:

> My hand brought *filmer Smith* to this strait bed —
> Well, fare his soul well, fear not I the dead.

She can be grim — but she won't stand for any nonsense about abandoning hope. That would be *ignoble*. In what looks like steps in a campaign against received "enlightened" opinion, she shows something of the terrifying honesty which Eliot ascribed to Blake. On one plane she seeks to rescue and rehabilitate the word "pretty." On another plane, "But Murderous" that begins:

> A mother slew her unborn babe
> In a day of recent date
> Because she did not wish him to be born in a world

Of murder and war and hate
"Oh why should I bear a babe from my womb
To be broke in pieces by a hydrogen bomb?"

takes an unexpected, heterodox turn: we are not invited to sym-
pathize with the mother and her "tragic dilemma," but rather
the opposite:

I say this woman deserves little pity
That she was a fool and a murderess
Is a child's destiny to be contained by a mind
That signals only a lady in distress?

And why should human infancy be so superior
As to be too good to be born in this world?
Did she think it was an angel or a baa-lamb
That lay in her belly furled?

At the very end there is, perhaps, another turn:

How foolish this poor mother to suppose
Her act told us aught that was not murderous
(As, item, That the arrogance of a half-baked mind
Breeds murder; makes us all unkind.)

Makes us *all* unkind—including the poet herself.

No, Miss Smith was not notably trusting. She didn't altogether trust the Muse. The Muse deserts you because you have
complained that she doesn't speak loudly enough—and you hear
her howling and muttering behind the door. Then you search by
night and day and cry upon the Lord to give her back to you:

He did repent. I have her now again
Howling much worse, and oh the door is open.
("Who Is This Who Howls and Mutters?")

The poet may be happy, healthy, in himself, but his poetry can be unhappy, distressing himself and others, as in "The Word":

> My heart leaps up with streams of joy,
> My lips tell of drouth:
> Why should my heart be full of joy
> And not my mouth?
>
> I fear the Word, to speak or write it down,
> I fear all that is brought to birth and born:
> This fear has turned my joy into a frown.

Not very trusting, but she was never cynical. And not hard so much as brisk, and especially brisk in situations which require briskness and a touch of bracing tartness. For all the dippiness, she was a moralist firm in degree and central in kind, and a moralist in the best sense, for she felt while she judged. The engaging combination of overt sternness with underlying gentleness is shiningly present in "Valuable" ("After reading two paragraphs in a newspaper"), which I quote in full:

> All these illegitimate babies . . .
> Oh girls, girls,
> Silly little cheap things,
> Why do you not put some value on yourselves,
> Learn to say, No?
> Did nobody teach you?
> Nobody teaches anybody to say No nowadays,
> People should teach people to say No.
>
> Oh poor panther,
> Oh you poor black animal,
> At large for a few moments in a school for young children
>   in Paris,
> Now in your cage again,
> How your great eyes bulge with bewilderment,
> There is something there that accuses us,

In your angry and innocent eyes,
Something that says:
I am too valuable to be kept in a cage.

Oh these illegitimate babies!
Oh girls, girls,
Silly little valuable things,
You should have said, No, I am valuable,
And again, It is because I am valuable
I say, No.

Nobody teaches anybody they are valuable nowadays.

Girls, you are valuable,
And you, Panther, you are valuable,
But the girls say: I shall be alone
If I say "I am valuable" and other people do not say it of me,
I shall be alone, there is no comfort there.
No, it is not comforting but it is valuable,
And if everybody says it in the end
It will be comforting. And for the panther too,
If everybody says he is valuable
It will be comforting for him.

Miss Smith wanted happiness to exist where it possibly could.
Indeed, whe would have liked to see Phèdre happily married to
Hippolytus: "I think it might have been a go. . . . " But life, she
knows, is a struggle, no matter what you might think you would
like it to be instead:

> Ceux qui luttent ce sont ceux qui vivent.
> And down here they luttent a very great deal indeed.
> But if life be the desideratum, why grieve, ils vivent.

And though she has asked—more precisely, "a little wind sneak-
ing along That was older than all and infamously strong" has
asked—"Will Man ever face fact and not feel flat?," in practice

man is often seen to rise superior to his myths. Even to the cruel story of Eve ("How Cruel Is the Story of Eve"):

> . . . there is this to be said still:
> Life would be over long ago
> If men and women had not loved each other
> Naturally, naturally,
> Forgetting their mythology
> They would have died of it else
> Long ago, long ago,
> And all would be emptiness now
> And silence.

Man sometimes does contrive to face fact and not fall flat on his face, even to live not without honor, so that on balance

> It is his virtue needs explaining,
> Not his failing.
>
> Away, melancholy,
> Away with it, let it go.
>
>   ("Away Melancholy")

As for eccentricity and quaintness, Miss Smith's themes are commonly the large ones, central to the human condition. Extremely interesting, and sufficient to dispose of any suggestion of her being a *naif*, are her reflections on death and suicide. The possibility, or the availability, of suicide is a great strengthener, Pompey muses; every child should be told, "Things may easily become more than I choose to bear" —

that "choose" is a grand old burn-your-boats phrase that will put beef into the little one, and you see if it doesn't bring him to a ripe old age. If he doesn't in the end go off natural I shall be surprised . . . See what it's done for me. I'm twice the girl I was that lay crying and waiting for death to come at that convalescent home. No, when I sat up and said: Death has got to come if I call him, I never called him, and never have.

And so, in the terms of one simple little verse, you look at the
bottle of aspirin when you feel mournful, you reflect that two
hundred will free you from anxiety—but you don't do more than
look. Death you should think of as a friend: though you can call
upon a friend, you should not impose upon him—and moreover
Death is also a "great prince." Miss Smith valued propriety and
decorum. The argument is by no means unsubtle. On the one
side,

> a time may come when a poet or any person
> Having a long life behind him, pleasure and sorrow,
> But feeble now and expensive to his country
> And on the point of no longer being able to make a decision
> May fancy Life comes to him with love and says:
> We are friends enough now for me to give you death;
> Then he may commit suicide, then
> He may go.

On the other side (as in "Mr. Over"), it may be a devil's voice
that cries, "Happy Happy the dead," for God says this:

> In man is my life, and in man is my death,
> He is my hazard, my pride and my breath,
> I sought him, I wrought him, I pant on his worth,
> In him I experience indeterminate growth.
>
> Oh Man, Man, of all my animals dearest,
> Do not come till I call, though thou weariest first.

Neville Braybrooke recalls Stevie Smith having said to him
towards the end of her life: "People think because I never married, I know nothing about the emotions. When I am dead you
must put them right. I loved my aunt." One could not for long
suspect her of such ignorance. She was no *cenobite*—to use one of
Pompey's favorite names for unfavorite things: "two diseases we
have right here that the modern world is suffering from — *dic-*

tators like I said and *cenobites* like I said too. . . . " In a short poem called "Man Is a Spirit," she points out snappishly that, even so, the spirit-guest oughtn't to wrinkle up his nose at the flesh-host who serves him well when the wind blows. And obviously she agrees with Ormerod when he maintains that he can have knowledge of God both before life and after death, but that here in temporal life, and only in temporal life, is permitted "A place where man might impinge upon man, And be subject to a thousand and one idiotic distractions" —

> I knew, and shall know again, the name of God, closer
>   than close;
> But now I know a stranger thing,
> That never can I study too closely, for never will it come again—
>
> Distractions and the human crowd.
>
>   ("Distractions and the Human Crowd")

There is a time and a place for everything. Ripeness is all, ripeness of time and rightness of place.

In its essence Stevie Smith's poetry is uncluttered, and hence must leave out, for instance, the reservations and modifications and clarifications which a denser and slower-moving writing admits. But it leaves out what it could not accommodate and still be the kind of poetry it is: and that is all it leaves out. A reader may well prefer other kinds of poetry, of course, but he cannot make out that her poetry is one of those other kinds which has somehow "gone wrong." When it succeeds, it obeys its own laws, and they are not unduly restrictive. At moments she is like a lot of other poets — I would add Hardy, de la Mare, Ogden Nash, Edward Lear, the creators of ballads, of hymns, of nursery rhymes, to those already noted — but finally, in the totality of her work, she is simply like herself. At the worst her poems are rather dull, and one asks "So what?": that is the way of failing of her kind of poetry. I think she fails surprisingly rarely, especially if we read the poems in bulk, when among themselves they provide their own qualifications and refine their arguments. To say this is to remind oneself that a part of her best work, at all events her most *own,* hasn't been touched on here. And simply because there seems to be nothing to say about it: children are likely to enjoy it unworryingly, it engages adults and yet leaves them baffled and a little uneasy. It is not amenable to interpretation or conducive to moralizing. And one thinks of Pompey's sharp remarks on clever talk about books and pictures and how "you want to keep very mum-o, and you want to keep the smarties off, oh yes they can read now, and very cunning they are the way they pick things up, very quick and cunning, much fiercer about it they are. . . . " Perhaps it is appropriate to end with one such poem, "Voices about the Princess Anemone":

> Underneath the tangled tree
> Lies the pale Anemone.
>
> She was the first who ever wrote
> The word of fear, and tied it round her throat.
>
> She ran into the forest wild
> And there she lay and never smiled.
>
> Sighing, Oh my word of fear
> You shall be my only dear.
>
> They said she was a princess lost
> To an inheritance beyond all cost.
>
> She feared too much they said, but she says, No,
> My wealth is a golden reflection in the stream below.
>
> She bends her head, her hands dip in the water
> Fear is a band of gold on the King's daughter.

1971

✳

That One Must Speak Lightly

MICHAEL TATHAM

It is likely enough that if some Catholic controversialist of the early seventeenth century had been discussing the merits of various contemporary poets he would have extolled Crashaw and Southwell, deplored Donne, and vacillated in his opinion of the obscurer Alabaster according to whether that gentleman was imprisoned in England for the faith or had returned to the Anglican church and a wife after differences with the Inquisition. Disparagement or approval would have been a matter of party loyalties; not of poetry. And, no doubt, in a time of adversity the position was honorable — or at least understandable — enough. Now, however, when there is no excuse for it, such a simplistic attitude to religious allegiance is almost certainly an important factor in accounting for the intellectual and emotional impoverishment of religious art—the trite sentimentality of so many repository artifacts; the clerical sneer that dismisses the work of Graham Sutherland because he has lapsed—as if the integrity of an artist depended on Easter Communion. (It would be interesting to know how many of the great figures of the Renaissance were certifiably in a state of grace.)

Thus it came about that in March 1971 we lost one of the very few religious poets of our day, and it is doubtful whether anyone noticed. Stevie Smith herself would not have been at all surprised. Many years earlier, in "Poor Soul, poor Girl!" she had joked:

132

I cannot imagine anything nicer
Than to be struck by lightning and killed suddenly crossing
    a field
As if somebody cared. [1]

What would have annoyed her — and quite justifiably too —
would have been any attempt to take advantage of her disappear-
ance by plucking her bones oh so devoutly from their resting
place and setting them up for latter-day relics. Certainly she
would have smiled a little wanly at any hint of a suggestion that
after all she was "one of us." And of course she would be quite
right to repudiate any such shifty practice. She will only be one
with us if we go out alone to find her, for there can be no shirking
the fact that in her eyes the face of the church was marked by a
terrifying cruelty and a contemptible dishonesty. In love she had
no choice but to turn away. Nevertheless—or even perhaps, because of this turning—Stevie Smith was a profoundly religious
poet and speaks to our condition as modern piety can seldom
hope to speak.

Neither, it has to be said, will fashionable reassurances of the
"we are all ecumenical now" variety help a dishonest cause;
Stevie Smith was nothing if she was not unfashionable—hers an
amusingly recusant soul . . . . Indeed, during the thirties and
forties, she had great difficulty in getting her poetry published, [2]
and not long before her death she remarked ironically, "Like anyone else that doesn't go to church I'm very much against
changes! [3] (How she would have loathed the new vernacular mass
—unless, perhaps, as some humorist suggested, the church had

1. All quotations in this article are from Stevie Smith, *Selected Poems* (London: Longmans, 1962) or *Scorpion* (London: Longmans, 1972), unless otherwise indicated.

2. "Poet on Thin Ice," an interview by John Horder, *Guardian* (7 June
1965):5.

3. John Gale, "Death Is a Poem to Stevie Smith," *Observer* (9 Nov.
1969):21.

the wit to refurbish the old Anglican service when the Church of England had finally discarded it). Poetically, her resistance to popularization found expression in the rather slight, "Why are the Clergy . . . ?" with its suitably astringent conclusion:

> Does Charity object to the objection?
> Then I cry, and not for the first time to that smooth face
> Charity, have pity.

In a somewhat similar piece of quasi-polemical verse (and inferior poetry), Stevie Smith demanded a proper recognition for the man who had created the great Anglican liturgy. As a writer, she insists in "Admire Cranmer," his touch was very much surer than that of his modern supplanters; and whatever our reservations about the archbishop, his masterful hypocrisy and time-serving pliability, there could be no room for doubting either the resonant beauty of his prose or the unexpected courage of his dying:

> Mocked by the priests of Mary Tudor, given to the flames,
> Flinching and overcoming the flinching, Cranmer.

But this too could easily become a false trail, for a shared if belated recognition of the archbishop's literary merits scarcely constitutes the sort of all-embracing ecumenical gesture that entitles any of us to appropriate such a refreshingly unecumenical perception. Only now, perhaps, in this present shallow time when — whatever we pretend — we mostly live without faith, is it quite in order for us to take whatever comfort we can from the fact that a religious poet is at one with us in our predicament. Prayer and God are perceived to be equally irrelevant to our material well-being. Not only is God never now about in the quad; but were someone to notice Him there after all, He would certainly be a very considerable moral embarrassment. Stevie Smith's remarkable achievement as a poet was to sustain a dialogue with God in which there was no pretense that a comfortable response was possible. As always wryly humorous she was to remark: "I wish I were more cheerful, it is more pleasant."

In another respect, Stevie was always a child of her time—of
the very best of her times—and since she was determined not to
be cosily cheerful so that evil might the more easily be glossed
over, much of her conversation, as in "Away Melancholy," was a
furious rejection of that appalling construction of human logic
and perverse ingenuity, the God made with human hands—the
Father of the inferno and the church militant . . . old Nobo-
daddy.

> Speak not to me of tears,
> Tyranny, pox, wars,
> Saying, Can God
> Stone of man's thought, be good?

There was never any doubt in Stevie Smith's mind that only
man's moral inadequacy permitted him to worship a deity of
whom he still believed it possible that—in Yvonne Lubbock's
words—"God resurrects some bodies solely in order to torture
them for ever."[4]

> So the vulnerable body is stretched without pity
> On flames for ever. Is this not pretty?

> The religion of Christianity
> Is mixed of Sweetness, for she wears
> A smoky dress out of hell fires.
> > ("Thoughts about the Christian
> > Doctrine of Eternal Hell")

Such a rejection was of course the easy bit, but if she was to be
a child of her times in this she also had to accept the corollary
that it would prove impossible to relocate the lost heaven of her
childhood imagery. In any case, heaven has always been a problem—a problem the old authorities preferred to fudge, "the eye
hath not seen," that sort of thing. In a recent novel,[5] W. J.

---

4. "Belief Is Being," in *The Future of Catholic Christianity* (London: Con-
stable, 1966).

5. *One of Our Priests Is Missing* (Harmondsworth: Penguin, 1968).

Weatherby sees heaven through the eyes of an elderly priest as a type of suburb—an image which may well owe something to the idea first put forward by C. S. Lewis in his *Great Divide* that heaven is a very superior municipal park which can be reached by bus from anywhere within the urban boundaries of hell. The Lewis model heaven is open to all who wish to stay there; but, hardly surprisingly, very few people can stand such a dull place. Stevie comes close to making the same point in "God Speaks."

> . . . I should like him to be happy in heaven here.
> But he cannot come by wishing. Only by being already at
>   home here.

Nevertheless, whatever the imagery, heaven remains difficult; compared with the well-documented geography of hell even the most cheerful of municipal parks lacks charisma. Small wonder, in fact, if the park remains comfortably empty and congregations continue to dwindle. Those pious forefathers who painted their lurid judgements on the walls of every country church knew what they were about; for we too have sat enthralled over our *Brighton Rock,* stared through the newsprint at the mutilated corpse, and remembered perhaps the missionary nuns who held a Eurasian girl's finger in a candle flame because she would not lie.[6] And of course if Heaven lacks much of the reassuringly familiar which we rightly associate with hell then love: St. Francis and St. Clare talking together in a nimbus of gold; Krishna dancing with Radha; Bernini's swooning Teresa—all intensely sexual icons—may well prove equally elusive. Stevie Smith was to write of love most often in terms of its contradiction—in terms that is of loneliness and isolation. Nowhere is this more apparent than in the restrained, ironic cadences of "Francesca in Winter" in which the torments of human passion—that burning unease—are seen sadly enough in terms of Dante's account of the Second Circle in Hell.

6. Jon Godden and Rumer Godden, *Two under the Indian Sun* (Melbourne: Macmillan, 1966).

O LOVE sweet love
I feel this love
It burns me so
It comes not from above

It burns me so
The flames run close
Can you not see
How the flames toss

Our souls like paper
On the air?
Our souls are white
As ashes are

O love sweet love
Will our love burn
Love till our love
To ashes turn?

I wish hellfire
Played fire's part
And burnt to end
Flesh soul and heart

Then we could sit beside our fire
With quiet love
Not fear to look in flames and see
A shadow move.[7]

Two of the shorter and frequently anthologized poems, "Not Waving but Drowning" and "I Remember," come close to saying all that need be said about our inescapable isolation from one another — that other face of love — and few lines are so hauntingly memorable as that poignant movement out of colloquial speech rhythms:

7. The final verse is omitted here.

> I do not think it has ever happened
> Oh my bride, my bride.

It is perhaps not surprising that Stevie should have shared Hardy's belief that almost the worst part of human relationships is to be found in our wretched capacity for "looking away," for failing to seize the moment of joy and for failing to respond to the desperate plea for recognition and understanding.

> Now when she cries, Father, Mother, it is only to please,
> Now the people do not mind, now they say she is a mild tease.

Stevie Smith's compassion is entirely consistent with John Horder's sketch in *The Guardian;* he remarked that she was "noticeably without the defence mechanisms or props that many poets adopt to keep the abyss at bay." Perhaps this is another way of saying, as Stevie does of herself, "I'm probably a couple of sherries below par most of the time."[8] It is entirely fitting that it is the dragon, Fafnir, who wins her sympathy rather than the victorious knight.

> I shall say then,
> Thou art better dead
> For the knights have burnt thy grass
> And thou couldst not have fed.

Perhaps not surprisingly just as Stevie Smith's virtue as a religious poet lies in her sharing of our anxieties and disbeliefs; so conversely, when she is most specifically religious, she is least successful. The probing hostility of her Christology in "Was He Married? appears to suffer from a looseness of treatment; the dialogue, despite its value as debate, is here entirely self-contained, and one senses a certain superficiality which is also apparent in the verse attacking Christian acceptance of slavery, "Was it Not

8. Gale, "Death Is."

Curious?" Perhaps only her "Airy Christ," inspired by reading Dr. Rieu's Penguin translation of St. Mark's Gospel, is as successful as a more conventionally religious poem can hope to be at this date. The first lines evoke sunlight pouring through great perpendicular windows of clear glass, while the final stanza reveals the same crystaline simplicity:

> For he does not wish that men should love him more than
> anything
> Because he died: he only wishes they would hear him sing.

Stevie Smith's treatment of prayer in "In the Park" is also remarkably satisfactory, and we are caught by the almost metaphysical inversion of meaning before we are fully aware of what has happened — the comedy of the confusion and misunderstanding becomes a joke against the reader.

The culmination of her more controversial religious poetry was probably the piece which the *Guardian* printed a few years ago at Whitsun.[9] It contained many of her recurring criticisms of Catholicism and touched on difficulties which must concern very likely a majority of thoughtful Christians. They are worth setting out in some detail.

1. That because the Holy Spirit is the inspiration of good even those who do not accept the Christian faith often feel they must keep silent "in case good suffers."

2. That somehow good must be separated from what is essentially, "A beautiful cruel lie, a beautiful fairy story."

3. That the Creation story can no longer be believed.

4. That Christian belief in the inspiration of scripture is now a valueless nonsense.

5. That Christ's redemption of mankind was a "dreadful bargain, that God would take and offer/The death of his Son to buy our faults away."

9. Afterwards called "How Do You See," published in *Scorpion*.

6. That Christians accept the appalling doctrine of eternal punishment.

Stevie goes on—ever more passionately—to implore the church:

> Oh what do you mean, what do you mean?
> You never answer our difficulties

before reverting to the point she had first developed years earlier in "Was He Married" that Christ could not be both God and man.

> If He was God He was not like us
> He could not lose.

From here she went on to question the mystery of the Trinity, the Holy Ghost, and the consolations offered by religion, "so beautiful, but not when you look close," and hence to castigate the Roman Catholic hierarchy endlessly discussing—

> Their shifty theology of Birth Control, the Vatican
> Claiming the inspiration of the Holy Spirit . . .

but, thanks to the power of the "Civil Arm," "kinder than it was." Stevie ends with a plea for honesty—"to be good without enchantment."

It was unfortunate that when Fr. Hill replied a few days later, ingeniously parodying her style; instead of acknowledging her very real problems, he chose to accuse her of bad faith. This was unwise for it demonstrated only too well that Stevie Smith's bewilderment and suspicion were well founded. It is too late in the day to say, "You are not a fair questioner or a fair listener," throwing in for good measure the well-worn charge of spiritual pride.

> I yearn for you, poor proud child of Europe,
> Because you will not believe, and you refuse

To believe because you pretend that you want to understand
But you do not really want to understand,
Because to understand you must be humble . . .

Not only was Fr. Hill, understandably, unable to supply answers; but far more disappointingly, he entirely failed to appreciate the true depth of her concern. Such failures tend to establish the critical case. More amusingly the correspondence printed beneath Fr. Hill's reply[10] was a useful guide to the intellectual and spiritual malaise which equates love of God with a set response of appropriately devout noises. Finally it was left to David Holbrook, writing as an agnostic, to ask more helpfully why truth should be obvious and to suggest that the problems of inner reality could only be explored by metaphor. In this respect, Stevie Smith's own attitude is not without ambiguity. One thinks of such lines as:

And I believe that two and two
Are but an earthly sum
Whose totalling has no part at all
In heavenly kingdom-come,

and the factually mournful counter refrain which accompanies it,

Ah me, the countless dead, ah me
The countless countless dead.

10. One doctor accused the *Guardian* of disliking Christianity and detesting Roman Catholicism. An Anglican suggested that having reached the sixth form Stevie Smith should know better than to confuse religious myth and fairy story. "And, Sir, it really sounds as if she had forgotten about her prayers." It is worth recalling Simone Weil's letter to the Dominican, Father Perrin: "During all this time of spiritual progress I had never prayed. I was afraid of the power of suggestion that is in prayer — the very power for which Pascal recommended it — Pascal's method seems to me one of the worst for attaining faith" (*Waiting on God* [New York: Harper and Row, 1973], 70).

My own sympathies are with Holbrook but I can see that there must be a temptation for us to prefer the indistinct latitudes of myth to the far less attractive limitations of "fact." And besides, for all Fr. Hill's play with the unfactualness of facts, it remains true that the Catholic church had given little encouragement to the view that her historical assertions may be understood metaphorically or symbolically. Eric Gill's somewhat selective autobiography provides a typical example:

> The burden of my song was that I accepted the whole metaphysical and philosophical basis of Catholicism but that when it came to the historical and physical matters — the Bible, the Gospel miracles, the Mass and all the rest of it — I didn't see how it could be acceptable except as symbolical. "Pas symbolique, pas symbolique," he kept on replying. [11]

Stevie Smith's Whitsun poem was perhaps most useful in revealing the sheer poverty of conventional religious responses to anything outside a well-defined intellectual frontier. How much better it would have been if instead of attempting to bludgeon her with assorted fathers of the church her passionate convictions and very real anxieties had been treated with the respect recently accorded to Epicurus (formerly bête noire of ignorant generations) by Fr. Festugière. [12] It is time for a glimmer of understanding. If the parable of the sheep and the goats is too familiar — and probably large parts of the gospels *are* too familiar — then Lear and Cordelia remain. Charlotte Mew in her poem, "Madeleine in Church, [13] or even the absurd Undershaft of *Major Barbara* [14] may tell us things which St. Matthew's Gospel fails to tell us. Simone Weil warns us that Christ likes us to prefer the truth to him — because "before being Christ he is truth. If one turns aside from him to go towards the truth, one will not go far

---

11. *Autobiography* (London: Jonathan Cape, 1940).
12. *Epicurus and His Gods* (Oxford: Basil Blackwell, 1955).
13. *The Farmer's Bride* (London: Poetry Bookshop, 1921).
14. Bernard Shaw, *Major Barbara* (Harmondsworth: Penguin, 1960).

before falling into his arms."[15] The problem is as sharp now as it was a quarter of a century ago, perhaps even sharper. There are few pages in such books as *The Future of Catholic Christianity*[16] which are not concerned with the difficulties raised by Stevie Smith, and the questions and doubts seem a good deal more relevant than the answers. Clearly this is not the place to pursue Miss Smith's objections much further, but it may be worth noticing a few lines from Simone Weil's *Letter to a Priest* which — predictably enough — had such a poor reception when it first came out — a reception largely due to the fact that it clearly dispelled the misconception that only Simone's early death prevented her from finding her way into the church.

> Everything has proceeded as though in the course of time no longer Jesus, but the Church, had come to be regarded as being God incarnate on this earth. The metaphor of the "mystical body" serves as a bridge between the two conceptions. But there is a difference, which is that Christ was perfect, whereas the Church is sullied by a host of crimes. [17]

It is such a distinction that makes it possible for a religious poet who has been brought up in the Christian tradition to write so angrily of the church.

On an entirely different and very much less important level, there is the minor critical problem of attempting to relate Stevie Smith's work to anything else in the same field. There is the danger possibly that if we are unable to see her work in the context of a school or tradition we may be tempted to dismiss it as somehow inconsequential and fey. To some extent this is a hazard faced by all religious poetry. In 1935 T. S. Eliot wrote: "when you qualify poetry as 'religious' you are indicating clear limita-

15. Weil, *Waiting*.

16. Lubbock, "Belief Is."

17. Simone Weil, *Letter to a Priest* (London: Routledge and Kegan Paul, 1953). An interesting example occurs in the *Aylesford Newsletter,* no. 42 (Apr. 1959).

tions. For the great majority of people who love poetry, Religious Poetry is a variety of minor poetry."[18] Something of this attitude — for all his disclaimer — is apparent in Patrick Dickinson's introduction to *Scorpion*. He calls Stevie a "Sunday poet," with a feeling for Sunday as opposed to other days of the week like a lapsed Catholic. He stresses her unique qualities and finds a comparison with Emily Dickinson — they both sprang from "a nowhere." More helpfully he observes, "Both shared a running quarrel with God in which God could seldom get in even an edgewise word." No doubt if Stevie Smith is really unique in the richest traditions of English eccentricity, we shall be obliged to accept Mrs. Malaprop's dictum that "Caparisons don't become a young woman," but if there is any doubt in the matter and we are to play the game of literary connections — however halfheartedly — there is no doubt that we shall find an echo of Hopkins in the last two lines of "In the Park."

> "Praise" cries the weeping softened one, "Not pray, praise,
>   all men,
> Praise is the best prayer, the least self's there, that least's release."

And absurd though it may seem to mingle comparisons so diverse there is surely also some odd, robust quality borrowed — who knows? — from the metaphysicals — some trace of Herbert in the line that begins a poem about the presence of God —

> Mother, among the dustbins, and the manure —

Yet it is to William Blake that I see the closest — but not of course too close — resemblance. Sometimes there is an echo — "It was a human face in my oblivion" — but more frequently the similarity is to be found in that deep concern for all sensitive life and an acute awareness of the blight that flies in the inescapable

18. T. S. Eliot, *Selected Prose* (London: Faber, 1951).

dark. There are the mutely anxious eyes of Pug and the travesty of love in "Over-Dew." And there is something too of Blake's vision of innocence in the recollected joy of "Archie and Tina":

Oh what pleasure, what pleasure!

There never were so many poppies as there were then,
So much yellow corn, so many fine days,
Such sharp bright air, such seas.

and in the lost Eden of her "Grateful Colours":

The grass is green
The tulip is red
A ginger cat walks over
The pink almond petals on the flower bed.

Perhaps also in the invocation to love which proclaims somewhat strangely, as Blake himself might well have done: "Votaries of Both Sexes Cry First to Venus."

But it is the message rather than the medium which must be our final concern, and it is clear in her last book that Stevie Smith had moved toward an acceptance of suffering and loss at least as powerful as any Christian hope. On the one side there is the heaven-approved epitaph of "Angel Boley," "She did evil that good might come," and on the other—

Grief spoke these words to me in a dream, I thought
He spoke no more than grace allowed
And no less than truth.

With the acceptance of suffering came a growing delight in the certain approach of death. It was an attitude which was to endorse her position as a religious poet. This new mood is established by the title piece of the collection:

> O Lord God please come
> And require the soul of thy Scorpion
>
> Scorpion so wishes to be gone.
>
> ("Scorpion")

And the final stanza of the book with its reiterated last line,

> Come Death — Do not be slow.

Fittingly enough she had written earlier that we should "Study to Deserve Death," and it was equally in keeping that in talking to John Gale on the occasion of receiving the Queen's Gold Medal for Poetry she should have remarked, "I do really think death will be absolutely marvelous. I don't think one could possibly enjoy life without death; one couldn't stand it; not only the pain, but the pleasure. If there wasn't death I think you couldn't go on."[19] It is equally typical that she should have wondered whether death should be Death or death—and decided that both were perhaps necessary. In similar vein, as we are reading her poem:

> My heart goes out to my Creator in love
> Who gave me Death as end and remedy

we smile as we remember that she observed how very easily it might have become, "Creator in law."

Who can doubt that Stevie Smith's rare gift as a religious poet was not only to sing of disbelief as our common religious experience but to laugh self-mockingly at so much seriousness.

1972, 1989

---

19. Gale, "Death Is."

＊

Of Absent Friends

MICHAEL HOROVITZ

The last time I saw Stevie Smith was at her little house in Palmers Green, which I always thought of as "Bottle Green" from her *Novel on Yellow Paper*—and this may have something to do with the fact that I invariably brought bottles of wine when visiting there. We usually got a bit tipsy (on one occasion we took a rowing boat out on the lake nearby and were nearly both "not waving but drowning") with the result that any motivation for the visit was set aside, or completely forgotten, in the meandering (and ultimately turtle) course of it. The purpose of this particular meeting had been to decide on some poems and pictures for what was then to be the twelfth birthday reunion issues of *New Deps*. She got as far as sorting through one playbox, and we agreed on these two drawings; she was sure there were poems to go with them, but we were too cheerful to continue peering and fishing in the other boxes of papers; we vowed to meet again as soon as the texts turned up, and spent a happy afternoon arguing and gossiping and reading our latest poems to each other. A few weeks after this my wife became pregnant, and Stevie had fallen ill — preoccupations which conspired against another rendezvous. Despite much pleasurable roaming through all of her twelve books, I've found no reference whatever to a *Worldly ear.* She had written to me, a propos of a sketch I sent her depicting a black swan and a white swan, "—The Black Goddess is the one for me": this was not long after the New Moon Carnival at Al-

147

Worldly ear, sketch by Stevie Smith.

bert Hall where she and Robert Graves (who'd recently published his book of that title) opened the proceedings. — So it
could be that this duskily colored lady is a companion or corollary to the more prim-and-proper-looking white-skinned *Muse*

Muse, sketch by Stevie Smith.

(—who is actually, in Stevie's original drawing, crayoned pinko-gray).

Her *oeuvre* includes a couple of Muses, at least, who strike me as apposite to these pictures. The second stanza of "My Muse" is

rather touching in its implication that the Goddess, like the
Queen of England, has no alternative, no separate options, but
to be a Muse, dependent for her raison d'être on her subjects' desire to be inspired:

> Why does my Muse only speak when she is unhappy?
> She does not, I only listen when I am unhappy
> When I am happy I live and despise writing
> For my Muse this cannot but be dispiriting.

— It also strikes me as the possible Creed of a *Worldly ear* in a
down-to-earth sense, and might befit a black woman in special
— i.e., she might be that much more inclined to send any Muse
packing in favor of seizing the day when happiness comes along
(even if it's only in the form of a Person from Porlock—even only
"Porson," whose "grandmother was a Warlock"). — And at the
same time she'd be well aware, as was Stevie, with Brecht—and
Angela Davis—that the person who calls herself "happy, has not
read the newspapers."

— "To School!" conjures up the emphatic aphoristic edges of
"English Blake" ("Thank God, I never was sent to school/To be
Flogd into following the Style of a Fool"): —

> Let all the little poets be gathered together in classes
> And let prizes be given to them by the Prize Asses
> And let them be sure to call all the little poets young
> And worse follow what's bad begun
> But do not expect the Muse to attend this school
> Why look already how far off she has flown, she is no fool.

Stevie took to the revivalist spirit of "Live New Departures" like
a sainted duck to water—a cygnet—indeed, come to think of
it, she *was* our Muse with a Worldly ear. Marie Peel wrote in
Books and Bookmen (June 1971), "One can see how immediate and
exciting she must have found the eruption of poetic happenings
in the sixties. She flourished in their openness and anarchy, and
by her readings contributed greatly to their value." She was as

knowledgeable as any of us (from long experience — though she sometimes seemed the youngest in heart of all) about the different impact different kinds of performance can induce. She never stooped to demagogy: at Albert Hall she responded to distant shouts of "Can't hear" and "Louder" with " — Come nearer then!" — and they did . . .

Many of her poems were written for specific tunes (largely from *Hymns Ancient and Modern* which she'd sing, frequently off-key — always mind-stilling. And whilst her reading and writing styles were inimitably her own, we never stopped learning from her — notably Libby Houston: listen to the satiric notes in their more formal chants, with repeated or variant refrains and tart, proverbial interjections (not evidenced by Libby's more recent personal poems in this issue tho'); to a lesser extent myself and probably also Anselm Hollo, George MacBeth, and even Robert Creeley, in their less obscurantist moods. Stevie demonstrated that pretty well anything can, given a basic sureness of touch, be incorporated in verse, including equivocal components of rhythm, tone, pitch, and subject matter in the same poem: archaic and slangy, fanciful and acidly naturalistic, lyric and narrative, colloquial and aureate, cadenced and unbound. She seemed to revel in poetic tightrope-walking — teetering perilously on the verge of the abysmally prosaic, ponderous postures of McGonagall, but never quite falling. Plain truths were brought home in intentionally spare no-nonsense terms, and dithering modern gentility is perfectly in order for the loftiest of themes, as in her "Idylls of the King": "King Arthur rode in another world/And his twelve knights rode behind him/And Guinevere was there/Crying 'Arthur, where are you dear?' " — A weather eye, and ear, for the ridiculous were substantiated by devastating social comment in dramatic monologues, dialogues, cameos, and parables which condensed entire novels — even lives — deftly, but not superficially, in a few lines: —

> Drugs made Pauline vague.
> She sat one day at the breakfast table

> Fingering in a baffled way
> The fronds of the maidenhair plant.
>
> Was it the salt you were looking for dear?
> Said Dulcie . . . .

—Stevie was a past-mistress at this genre of thumbnail scenario, which overlapped so closely with the area many of us were into at that time, to wit—high-spirited exploration of the way people actually talk and behave, and irreverent speculations regarding the consequences. With the distinction that she was wont to endow her glimpses with more liberal helpings of compassion:

> Dear little Bog-Face,
> Why are you so cold?
> And why do you lie with your eyes shut?—
> You are not very old.
>
> > I am a Child of this World,
> > And a Child of Grace,
> > And Mother, I shall be glad when it is over,
> > I am Bog-Face.
> >
> > ("Bog-Face")

— The squibs and vignettes of [George] Brown, [Ivor] Cutler, [Spike] Hawkins, and [Roger] McGough are better enjoyed (as they were, in the round) in the light of this canon—as well as those of Spike Milligan, Edward Lear, de la Mare, and Lewis Carroll, archetypal originators all. But another distinction is that Stevie often had a strong moral, if not moralizing, impetus —a didactic sting in the tail, like a sibylline Jane Austen in reproof; and her targets surely earned it — as for instance "The Choosers" (which again, could almost have been an analogue for Adrian Mitchell's subtly taunting "Hear the Voice of the Critic" —"There are too many colours . . . ,"—self-approbating tastemakers on the old-boys' network:

> Oh we are the Choosers, what we say goes.
> . . . .

Hey ho what a merry game,
It is as if we were still in Pop, it is the same.

With a hey-ho and a yah
No, we will not have So-and-So
Because we do not like his hat or his Ma.

Outside of this eclectic and up-to-date circle
Slink the sleek Great Ones, and you know
They may go and not care a particle
Because the Angel of Posterity has chosen them
And the Choosers will not be known then,
All the same it is a shame to treat them so.

Let Posterity-Time come
Quicky and Choosers be dumb.

Oh why does England cherish her arts in this wise,
Picking inferiorly with grafted eyes?
It is because it is like the school they never forget,
So-and-so must be the driven out one, this the pet.

It was difficult not to marvel at how tough and robust Stevie remained in body as in mind — considering what a frail figure she cut, her delicacy exaggerated by the dolly-bird frocks and bar-strapped shoes she still donned, all through her sixties, for any sort of outing.[1] She told Kay Dick (who transcribed the conversation in *Ivy and Stevie* — Duckworth, 1971) of her surprise that "the young like my poems. I say to them, 'I can't see what

1. One unforgettable escapade we shared was a harbinger of the Kulchural Common Market, when (in the summer of 1967) I was invited to bring a visitation of poets, troubadors, and musicians to Brussels, as part of a "British Week" — very strange, with fully transplanted pubs, Morris Dancers, and a resplendently gleaming London bus negotiating its earnest path in and out of incredulous Tour-de-Belge cycling hordes. The organizers set us up in a luxury hotel where, straight after landing, our twelve-strong flying squad was confronted with a sumptuous banquet and seemingly unlimited alcoholic hospitalities. By the time the troupe's composite body was decanted (by a special coach) to a palatial concert hall for our evening recital, most of us were in

Stevie reading at the Royal Albert Hall, London in 1966.

you see in them, because on the whole they're a bit deathwards in their wish . . . ' and I should have thought that the attitude of the young was more courageous than mine — not that there's much difference between youth and age."

Notwithstanding the many affinities, Stevie also character-ized and delineated some of the differences: in the late poem, for instance, about a "retired donkey,/After a life-time . . . /Be-

---

extremely good voice, not least Stevie — whose nose was liable at the best of times to bristle for a snifter, on the rationale that she generally arrived "a cou-ple of sherries below par"!

Yet I had to tremble for her on that veritable roiling *bateau ivre,* with such a wild and woozy bunch in attendance. Bert Jansch, John Renbourn, [Adrian] Mitchell, [George] Brown, and myself were chanting and cackling in our cups, whilst [Anselm] Hollo was the most roaring drunk of all, disgorging on the couch what sounded to us like Viking battle cries — tho' he claimed later that they were innocuous Finnish ale-shanties (albeit given an extra di-mension by the maniacal clog-dance he executed in obbligato). It was our turn to be incredulous when, collapsed onstage at a long white-cloth'd table, we

Not reading at the Palais Voor Schoone Kunste, Brussels in 1967, sketch by Michael Horovitz.

encountered still more food and drink, plus a side table festooned with an additional array of wines and spirits! If I dare trust my memory at this point, the scene — virgin at first with epicurean promise, quickly and shamelessly dissolved into a boisterous re-take on Buñuel's "peasant's revolt" parody of Leonardo's *Last Supper* . . . Brian Patten immediately fell asleep, hunched in his fluffy off-white sheepskin coat, head lolling on a dish like some primeval offering, to rear up out of its stupor at intervals during the soirée (metamorphosing into the Dormouse from Alice) and inquire, "Have I read yet?"

Apart from Frances [Hooker Horovitz], Stevie was the only reader whose tween the shafts of regular employment/now free to go merry-making," she detects "in its eyes such a gleam/As is usually associated with youth/But it was not a youthful gleam really,/But full of mature truth./ . . . And of the hilarity that goes with age." Then again, she had written, in "To Carry the Child" ("into adult life/Is to be handicapped"):" — The poor child, what can he do,/Trapped in a grown-up carapace,/But peer outside of this prison room/With the eyes of an anarchist?"

— If death spelled demangelic deliverance for Mark Hyatt, it was something similar for Stevie from a longer view, looked to as an old acquaintance who'd always get house space ("because he is a scatterer . . . /He scatters the human frame/The nerviness and the great pain/Throws it on the fresh fresh air/And now it is nowhere); and as an ally whose advent was more philosophically awaited (" — Study to deserve Death. . . . /Prate not to me of suicide/Faint heart in battle, not for Pride/I say Endure, but that such end denied/Makes welcomer yet the death that's to be died — ") from a less wantonly structured saga of suffering and deprivation. She's described how " — As a baby I almost died . . . Just after I'd been born, poor Daddy took one look at me and rushed away to sea," and (as her "House of Mercy" poem has it)

> — Nor sent them money, nor came home again
> Except to borrow back

---

delivery contrived, in the end, to achieve a resonance apparently untouched by the overall liquefaction. She'd kept her good-humored mien throughout, distractedly doodling caricatures of retrograde cats and grisly gendarmes on the tablecloth, until it dawned on her that we were carousing and rollicking under the spotlit scrutiny of thousands of Belgians. She conveyed this discovery in stage whispers to the others, some of whom had already noticed: what none of us could more than dimly discern was how the audience were reacting to our unrehearsed *theatre absurde* — It seemed we were seen but imperfectly heard — seemed likely indeed, we glumly inferred, that many of them couldn't follow a word of the fractured wells of English we slurred, and that *Merde* to the tableau (increasingly blurred) was a view on which most of the

Her Naval Officer's Wife's Allowance from Mrs. S.
Who gave it him at once, she thought she should. . . .

I was the younger of the feeble babes
And when I was a child my mother died
And later Great Aunt Martha Hearn Clode died
And later still my sister went away . . .

When she was eight in a convalescent home, the hitherto doting maid suddenly got bored and jilted her—and so on, bearing up against recurrent bouts of ill-health, till her final Devon journey to take care of the sister, who'd had a stroke, and her own subsequent hospitalization there with an inoperable brain tumor. And yet, so far from inducing morbid neuroses, all this inarguably "great pain"—when it wasn't lethally desolating—clothed her in an armature she relished: "Now I am strong and lapped in sorrow/As in a coat of magic mail and borrow/From Time today and care not for tomorrow."

The kindly instincts and delights of innocence must have counterbalanced some of the bruised and poisoned fruits of her shadow side. But Stevie maintained the shrewd honesty, as well as the capacity for exultation, of a wise child. Hence her earthy acceptance from the first of divinity, as of mortality, in the everyday (and, at times, even the banal):

---

house concurred. Their admission receipts were footing the bill, and the Organizers' faces looked suddenly ill . . . Then, when all hope had gone, Stevie went on — and riotous hoots of applause occurred — she was convinced she was getting the bird, and begged leave to "stand down" — to vacate the dais for some other clown — A man of plaster, I was still ringmaster — she the Grace who'd avert a total disaster: so, with heart beating faster, I intrepidly clasped her
hand
    and
led her out to the mikes again, where she stood defiant as a tragedienne . . .
till the storms of clapping and whistling abated—whereupon she trilled like

Mother, among the dustbins and the manure
I feel the measure of my humanity, an allure
As of the presence of God. I am sure

In the dustbins, in the manure, in the cat at play,
Is the presence of God, in a sure way
He moves there. . . .

She wrote about religion, and affliction, with much fresh air
about her—a forthrightness, stoicism, and irony unprecedented
for me except by Beckett—of whose people hers occasionally remind me. The dustbin-"bottled" parents of *Endgame,* for instance (—"NAGG: Can you hear me?—NELL: Yes. And you?—
NAGG: Yes. (*Pause*). Our hearing hasn't failed. — NELL: Our
what? — ") dovetail with the abrupt closure of her Rapunzel's
lover's mating call: " — What's that darling? You can't hear
me?/That's odd. I can hear you quite distinctly". . . . Beneath
the surface gaiety there prowls her constant of high seriousness
— sometimes as humbly sacramental as George Herbert: " — I
too have felt the presence of God in the broom/I hold, in the cob-
webs in the room/But most of all in the silence of the tomb." —
And from this solace too, she must needs move on, and switch
back, and renew her criticism of life —

---

a song thrush, elated, and the ship thought sunk was rehabilitated.

I'm uncertain even now as to all the goofs and glories of that night, but as
far as Stevie was concerned, she was bravely outfacing a derisive mob, which
might just have been what they were applauding. I suppose, unless — with
more justice still — it was the astonishing unimpeachable fact of her. Hence
my sketch over the page, salvaged from the whirlpool of stoned scribblings in
my notebook of that trip (tho' it hardly begins to account for her appearance,
let alone her essence — whether Bacchic in Brussels or regal at the Ritz, or
ritzy at the Regal or the church bazaar, this tended to feel imminently larger
than life, a long-lost amalgam of Wicked Aunt, White Witch, Fairy God-
mother, and much else.

Somehow transported back to the hotel, after all manner of analyses, apol-

Ah! but that thought that informs the hope of our kind
Is but an empty thing, what lies behind?—
Naught but the vanity of a protesting mind

That would not die. . . .

Her faith is real, but her good sense brooks no hubristic or eva-
sive mystification. Nor would Stevie's reverence for "everything
that lives" put up for long with explanatory systems, however
orderly—not excepting "this Christian religious idea" she ber-
ated now for its inconsistencies, now for being "too tidy, too tidy
by far. In its extreme tidy logic . . . a diminution and a lie."—
Marie Peel confirms that "Morally she found it quite inadmissi-
ble, the mixture of sweetness and cruelty," which aroused her
emancipated and "many-layered apprehension." And Calvin Bedient, in his study of *Eight Contemporary Poets,* speaks of "tran-
scendent joy thwarted by circumstance or some . . . Original
Contradiction," pinpointing the unresolved discord between her
"classical scepticism and romantic liberation. Smith was open to
every likelihood and perhaps finally partial to none."
    —Certainly the inborn will to believe was tempered by her
sardonic intelligence, realism, and self-knowledge. Hers was a
vivacity "hungry to be interrupted/And bring my thoughts to an
end," rather than the fag of (re)construction, mythic artifice, sal-
vation, on the scale of anything like the Blakean Marriage of
Contraries. She'd more likely anticipate their incompatibility or

---

ogies, apoplexies, and assignations (or were they assassinations?) Frances and
I repaired to Stevie's room to wish her sweet dreams. Though embedded in
French translations of Agatha Christie, propped against banks of bleached
pillows in floral Victorian nightcap and gown, she welcomed us with the glee
of a schoolgirl at an unlooked-for midnight feast, her tiny frame subsumed by
osmosis (like the Cheshire Cat) under that familiar conspiratorial grin, ex-
uding indomitable reserves of bonhomie and perennial spirit
                    So in a voice, so in a shapelesse flame,
                    Angells affect us oft, and worship'd hee . . .

divorce — *and* celebrate it in verses which played them off, by virtue of a decidedly unfair share of Negative Capability . . . Where a recognition such as Blake's *"Divine Image"* — "Cruelty has a Human Heart,/And Jealousy a Human Face;/Terror the Human Form Divine" — drew him toward an alternative all-encompassing synthesis, she was more inclined to record — to deplore and to embrace — the disunity she saw.

This was valid, for all that it was chastening, and seen "with, *not* through the eye": "It is a human face that hides/A monkey soul within" — which, "peering forth, will flesh its pads,/And utter social lies./So wretched is this face, so vain/So empty and forlorn,/You well may say that better far/This face had not been born." And in "Will Man Ever Face Fact and Not Feel Flat?" she hears "an angel call":

> The tender creature needeth love,
> He needeth love above all.
>
> This made the rocks and trees laugh more
> Until they saw the force of it,
> Saw Man disembowelling the earth
> And Killing because of it.

An actual dumb ape, on the other hand, who clambers astride the garden swing, elicits Stevie's unreserved lyricism (to the melody of "Green-sleeves"!) — "Oh ho the swinging ape,/The happy peaceful animal,/Oh ho the swinging ape,/I love to see him gambol."

— The beauties and beasts (and uglies), including human ones, for whom her poems and drawings provide sympathetic testimony, are legion, ranging from the sloshed "Jungle Husband" writing home ("Yesterday I hittapotamus . . . "), to her "Alfred the Great": "Honour and magnify this man of men/Who keeps a wife and seven children on £2 10/Paid weekly in an envelope/And yet he never has abandoned hope"; the "Friends of the River Trent (At Their Annual Dinner)":

A dwindling body of ageing fish
Is all we can present
. . . .
Because of water pollution, my boys,
And a lack of concerted action,
These fish of what they used to be
Is only a measly fraction
A-swimming about most roomily
Where they shoved each other before,
Yet not beefing about being solitary
Or the sparseness of the fare.
Then three cheers for the ageing fish, my boys,
Content in polluted depths
To grub up enough food, my boys,
To carry 'em to a natural death,
And may we do the same, my boys,
And carry us to a natural death.

—to the "Poor chap, he always loved larking". . . . except—

Nobody heard him, the dead man
But still he lay moaning:
I was much further out than you thought
And not waving but drowning.

— And from Helen of Troy, Gretchen, and Phèdre reborn, to "The Debutante" ("I cannot imagine anything nicer/Than to be struck by lightning and killed suddenly crossing a field") and other gals "on the shelf" — and fellahs in extremis to boot: "— I hate this girl/She is so cold,/And yet her eyes say/She is not as good as gold,/I should like to kill her,/But what do I do?/Kiss her, kiss her,/And wish that she would kiss me too." Stevie's deepest affections are extended to the misused, rejected, and misunderstood, whose secret lives and extenuating circs are nobly articulated and championed — the deepest inspirited from her Muse, anyway: — whilst "Happiness is like England, and will not state a case,/Grief like Guilt rushes in and talks apace."

The confluence of life-force with death wish was, like the other quarrels with herself, a reflection of her metaphysical completeness; they were necessary polarities of the whole truth, as she experienced it. She confided to Kay Dick:

> There's a terrible lot of fear of life in my poems. I love life. I adore it, but only because I keep myself well on the edge . . . I'm very ashamed of it, but there it is, dear. I love death . . . As one gets older one gets into this — well, it's like a race, before you get to the waterfall, when you feel the water slowly getting quicker and quicker, and you can't get out, and all you want to do is to get to the waterfall and over the edge.

The last poem she wrote, and the only one left unpublished was "Come Death" — in her usual "really interested" speaking voice, its burden pared and worn down to the barest simplicity of address:

> I feel ill. What can the matter be?
> I'd ask God to have pity on me,
> But I turn to the one I know, and say:
> Come, Death, and carry me away.
>
> . . . .
> Listen then to this sound I make, it is sharp,
> Come Death. Do not be slow.

One of Stevie's most valuable legacies to the *Children of Albion* and kindred poets is this compulsive directness (—surviving its adoption as a mask), the still unfashionable notion that anyone might look into his heart and write — and well, so he speak straight and true what's there.

— The sharp sound will be ringing in the ears of all who ever heard her poems — for many moons in many rooms, twixt book and bed, hearth and head, thought and deed — with echoes of their outrageous, universal, implacable observations.

There are some human beings who do not wish for eternal life, sketch
by Stevie Smith.

This page from her published sketchbook (*Some Are More Human Than Others*—Gaberbocchus, 1958) may seem initially a far
cry from Hyatt's proposition in his dying utterance ("Border
Line"); but since it surely refers to life (as) on this planet, it could

be understood as a less melodramatic, a breezier and more paradoxical, acknowledgment of a proximate (again, Beckettian) theology. And especially so when taken in conjunction with the following remarks — in answer to Kay Dick's checking, "But you wouldn't like to be dead, would you?"—

> Yes, I think it must be marvelous. Well, it might be something rather nice. I don't know . . . What pulls one up from these terrible depressions — it's the thought that it's in your own hands, that you can if you want to, make an end of it, but one never does. Some people do, obviously, but I've been more fortunate. I'm supposed to be an agnostic, but I'm sort of a backslider as a believer, too. I mean I'm a backslider as a non-believer, because every now and then I think, "No, I have this feeling that . . . — well, it really comes in the Lord's Prayer, which of course is the most wonderful thing that's ever been said at the end, and people sort of gabble it off who don't really think what it means. Then it suddenly strikes one what it does mean — that last bit, "Thine is the Kingdom, the Power and the Glory," it's absolutely marvelous. It means that absolute good, absolute good, is in control of everything. Therefore of course one longs to die, because it would be more in control there than here, because being alive is like being in enemy territory. I think one feels that this ultimate good, God, has abdicated his power in this world. There, you'll feel at home — that's what Heaven is, and of course I have written a lot about that too.

Ms. Dick reports that a week after their interview Stevie "was beginning to have dizzy fits," and that "She died, almost serenely one was told, on Sunday, March 7, 1971"—i.e. only four months later. According to Peter Kiddle, who tried to help by visiting her regularly during the last few weeks, she nonetheless hated taking leave of her senses — and being seen to do so. The poem overleaf outlines some of his tribulation. As to hers, well — in a critique of spiritualism she wrote—

If you believe in God, you will let the dying go, glad that the pain of loss is ours, not theirs. They have finished with the imperfections of human love, its dark places of egoism, greed, and idolatry. And as even the new-born baby, with a full span of life ahead, cannot really be said to have to live very long, is it asking too much that we should love our dead and leave them alone, waiting for our own deaths to know what it is all about? Or to know nothing ever again.

Horace and Modernism

CALVIN BEDIENT

Of the many other "Horatian" volumes published during the year, at once the most brilliant and monumental is Stevie Smith's *Collected Poems*. Here, from an unlikely quarter, is an exemplification and indeed vindication in modern terms of the Latin virtues. For Smith (that eccentric jauntily named after a popular jockey) might well scandalize a Horace. On the other hand she is faithful to the modestly noble spirit of his poetics — faithful in her fashion.

Consider her genius for a great and simple — great because simple — style. Consider her power of pithy and direct statement. Consider her wit and mordant nuance. And consider the whiplashed craft of her poems: poems devoid of aesthetic or emotional overreaching, knowing their own size and weight precisely; poems, all the same, of stinging impact.

Consider, too, how easy and familiar she is, how conversational. If her tongue ran to old idioms, still her poems ring with common speech and have an almost runaway contemporary nervousness (ranging from neurotic to neurodynamic, always quirky and prompt and intense). Becoming, inventing various attitudes, she acts with the voice, whether wickedly, as in "Does Charity object to the objection?/Then I cry, and not for the first time to that smooth face/Charity, have pity," or bemusedly, as in "Black March":

I have a friend
At the end
Of the world.
His name is a breath

Of fresh air.
He is dressed in
Grey chiffon. At least
I think it is chiffon.
It has a
Peculiar look, like smoke.

Stevie Smith, with her flippant speed, her guerrilla tactics, Horatian? To be sure, she mocked and teased with the truth; still it was the truth she served. Like the Horace of ode 1:25 or 2:14 (the latter, by the way, superbly translated by [Charles] Sisson in *In a Trojan Ditch*), she delighted in giving the truth bite, and who is to say she delighted too much? She is always piquant as against sensational, having learned to "speak lightly, and use fair names like the ladies/they used to call/The Eumenides."

True, she skittered among the feelings, by no means all of them "nice," with what resembles rococo decadence—and skeptical, theatrical, weary she was. Yet this was but the partial result of her intention to let nothing human elude her. Serially, brilliantly, she played out almost all our possibilities, a fearless and therefore fearful mime. She put on scattiness, she performed anxiety, she was a murderer, a masochist, an innocent, an orphan, a bitter or fond or melancholy mother, a drunk, a condemned man, a loner, a looney, Persephone, the frog prince, Saint Anthony — what have you; she dramatized hatred but no less beatitude, admiration of courage, loyalty, tenderness, faith. If she rocked about, it was from a weighted base of wholesome confidence, and in a spirit compounding stern revelation with creative fun. She had sanity; she had balance.

All Stevie Smith's virtues are Latin except the one that may count most with Americans: that of being, withal, a poetic nonconformist sui generis. Here, as perhaps in her emotional free-lancing, the virus of modernism shows up in an otherwise Horatian artist — in her slightly feverish originality. Original she may unstoppably as well as felicitously have been; but at those moments when she strains for oddity, proving silly in the modern sense while aiming to be silly in the old, one sees that she thirsts for individuality. And so she is Horatian and yet not, as a glove turned inside out is the same glove and yet not, all "wrong."

Nonetheless her frequent triumph — and this is the larger point — was precisely to make eccentricity serve her subjects, her bold intentions. Mostly she knew full well that she herself was "not important." She was habitually severe both toward the truth and toward her art. Crowd her into a word and she is classical.

1977

*

Stevie Smith and the Untruth of Myth

STEPHEN WADE

There is a short poem by Stefan Doinas, the Romanian poet, in which he tells of "The poet as snow-merchant." It is a sort of parable which revolves around a myth of poet as enlightener. This is a rare poem nowadays for it uses a folklore myth; and I think that, since Yeats, poets generally have thought of myth as being gigantic, consequential, and significant. It has been seen as a meaningful allegory of the modern psyche and so on. Now, for me, the poets who have used myth in less grand ways have given more stimulation; the "Byzantium" of Yeats is all very well, but there is a need to simplify now, I believe, and though I could write ten pages of criticism on "Sailing to Byzantium," I would rather look at more recent and less celebrated attempts to do justice to myth in poetry.

One could mention writers like [Edward] Brathwaite and [Nathaniel] Tarn and go to cultures whose myths have come into poetry as a by-product of the new interest in anthropology and the rediscovery of *The Golden Bough,* but I would like to look at a personal and quirky use of myth in poetry — that by Stevie Smith, who has been rather overlooked by critics, but not now by the drama. Before I look at some of her poems, I would like to mention the views of two writers who have a bearing on Smith's use of myth: Charles Olson and David Jones. They both see myth as a form that should not only keep to the original meaning, "Talk, story, etc.," but also extend into an allegory with a particularly modern relevance. Jones, in his scholarly way, intellectualizes here, in the preface to *The Anathemata:*

> Whether there is a radical incompatibility between the world of myths and the world of the "formulae," or whether it is a matter only of historic accident, of an unfortunate and fortuitous association of ideas leading to estrangement and misunderstanding, are questions which are continually debated.

This statement is, for me, the central one in any talk of myth in modern poetry. If one applies this remark about the "estrangement and misunderstanding" in this context to Smith's "Fafnir and the Knights" for example, one sees that the great difficulty which Jones refers to is one of uniformity of all readers' response. Jones himself overcame this by making his "sigma" only too well indicated in footnotes and elaborate explanations, and of course, these are needed for his poetry. On the other hand, Stevie Smith is the kind of poet who needs all her allegory to be implied and also "open" to various interpretations. Fafnir may be all things to all readers.

Charles Olson, in *The Human Universe,* refers to the split in the Western mind since the Ancients, of logical explanation and immediate action. He concludes that art must not describe, but act. Now, the use of myth in poetry enables the poet to omit all comment, all description. Yeats could not leave out the comment. He could not forget himself, the author's interposing voice. I would argue that recent poets have perceived that myth may be more than a religious dimension but also less than a metaphorical explanation of some part of man that will always be eternal, cyclical, and evident in all societies. Just as Sir James Frazer searched for the factual evidence of belief in myth all the world over, so poetry had the potential to exploit myth in all forms from the local and superstitious to the universal. Olson thought that the allegory of myth could be said but left alone.

In my view, this is where we begin with Stevie Smith; with the "open allegory" that treats of old myth. It is a good thing to bear in mind the meaning of "allegory" here — "To speak . . .

other." That word, "other" is the vital one for Smith. In her famous miniature poem, "Croft," she relies entirely on that unsaid "other" for effect:

> Aloft,
> In the loft,
> Sits Croft;
> He is soft.

It is a meditation which works entirely by suggestion, and its success depends on whether the implications expand in the reader's mind. As Tyrone Guthrie said, "It is one of the paradoxies of art that a work can only be universal if it is rooted in a part of its creator which is most privately and particularly himself." Yet, if we admit the close link between myth and allegory, we must see in Smith's poetry all the more power in mythology because of the absence of any overt explanation of the casual background. In the Fafnir poem, she is expressing something similar to Jung in this passage from *Memories, Dreams, Reflections*.[1]

> I had written a book about the hero, the myth in which man has always lived. But in what myth does man live nowadays? In the Christian myth, the answer might be. "Do you live in it?" I asked myself. To be honest, the answer was no . . . I had reached a dead end.

Jung is suggesting that it is not the individual who resists or loses his mythology, but that the mythology has to be part of a world picture shared by a large group of people. For Stevie Smith, there will be many versions of how Fafnir came to die. It is left to us. She has reached a dead end too:

> Fafnir, I shall say then,
> Though art better dead
> For the knights have burnt thy grass
> And thou couldst not have fed.

1. C. G. Jung, *Memories, Dreams, Reflections* (New York: Pantheon, 1963). 171.

Of course, Smith sees the idea of myth as any accepted exemplary ideal behind any kind of belief, and it is one of her favorite poetic styles to explore these. "Was He Married?" is this process with the life of Jesus. She seems to demythologize him — "Did he never feel strong/Pain for being wrong" and so on, but one feels that she would do the same for any archetype of belief or dogma.

For this reason, my reading of Smith's use of mythology is that she somehow made many variations of mythology, a series of explorations which turned in on herself—as a typically ordinary person. (Ordinary in her supposed attitudes on the printed page at least.) This inwardness when she uses myth in her poems is what gives them this open-ended nature. If one reads, say, Well's *The Time Machine,* and thinks of the allegory of the Eloi and the Morlocks, there are a lot of factors which point to a single, definite, demarcated reading of the allegory. The detail is all there. Smith, on the other hand, keeps nothing but her identification with YOU there. By this means, a myth can stay in its proper dimensions and yet still be meditated upon and used in a hundred different ways.

By using humor, absurdity, repetition, and patternless lines ending in rhymes, Stevie Smith convinces us that myth is no more than a fascinating untruth—or perhaps half-truth.

One conclusion from her style is that she is saying that myths now must have personal significance, just as our religions must. Smith explores, through her personality and with a "typical," playful enquiry, the implications of myths, in the widest sense of the word. The stories of Jesus, King Arthur, and the person from Porlock all assume a position of parity, as regards their nature of half-truth or untruth.

My personal view of her work of this type is that she sees all secondhand forms of knowledge as being significant, not for the "mass" any longer, but for the interpretation of the mass's intellectual limitations or emotional deficiency. When she considers the person from Porlock or Arthur or Fafnir, it is the use of "We," as in "May we inquire the name of the person from Porlock?" I think she is teaching us to question what I can only call the inwardness of myth. The way it works within itself and in a pattern of meaning that is entirely its own. The best example in Smith's work is her poem, "The Blue from Heaven," where her comically serious rhymes need no reference to other elements of the Arthurian myth other than Guinevere and a few nameless knights. Her intention is to isolate one image and let the reader absorb this without the distraction of being reminded of what the details of Arthur's nature were in any one version.

The image of "Blue cornflowers" and other blue substances isolate a side of Arthur that the myths overlook — his ordinary love of being alone with his thoughts and not caring about dragons — being, in Stevie Smith's view, rather romantic. Of course, Stevie Smith also satirizes the myth as handled by Malory et alia, when she says of the knights,

> And the falling-off of Arthur
> Becomes their theme presently.

Naturally, Smith's explorations of myth have a playful side, as in her "River God of the River Mimram" poem; but as always, she uses a common fairy tale or legend to inspect or dissect received ideas, ranging from dogma to allegory. For me, she has made modern poets see that there is another way to treat myth, other than the overtly intellectual, and still keep the reader's mind on edge with enquiry. In a way, it is all a teasing of our literary and religious heritage in the sphere of folktale and myth, but it also provokes as it entertains. In an interview with Peter Orr, Stevie Smith once said that theology was a passionate interest of hers; and one can see that the nature of these poems on myth, like the ones on Christianity, is one of a relationship not unlike the Fool taunting and provoking Lear.

Stevie Smith's poetry includes myth as one more great, overawing force in life that is totally unfamiliar and has to be made more familiar and therefore less daunting by means of art. Perhaps there is no better instance of this than the opening of one of her most famous poems, "Scorpion," where,

> This night shall thy soul be required of thee

with its unordinary syntax very threateningly placed first, becomes,

> Will my soul be required of me tonight perhaps?

As in all the poems I have mentioned, here the overemphasis of the familiar and ordinary cuts all untruth down to size.

1977

Why Stevie Smith Matters

MARK STOREY

One of the oddest things about Calvin Bedient's extremely odd book, *Eight Contemporary Poets,* which landed on a surprised world in 1974, is the inclusion of Stevie Smith in his hagiographical roll call of significant modern poets (along with Charles Tomlinson, Donald Davie, R. S. Thomas, Philip Larkin, Ted Hughes, Thomas Kinsella, and W. S. Graham). Although Stevie Smith was awarded the Queen's Medal for Poetry in 1969 and although her *Collected Poems* were published handsomely by Allen Lane in 1975, she can hardly be said to have established herself in the communal or critical consciousness as much more than an eccentric, suitable material for a stage show, a poor Englishwoman's version of Emily Dickinson. Calvin Bedient acknowledges this eccentricity whilst at the same time postulating a chain of tradition, which runs from Larkin, through all the poets he discusses, including Stevie Smith, "right down into the gorge of modernism." If this seems like a classic case of a critic wanting to have his cake and eat it, we should not be surprised: Bedient's judgments are alternately willful, extravagant, and contradictory. It is very hard to know precisely what he is claiming for his poets, so rhapsodical and capricious is his approach; and it is characteristic that he should conclude his essay on Stevie Smith with this drool of stratospheric saliva:

> She knew perhaps everything the emotions can know with a
> knowledge as heavy as the earth and a brilliance as light as the

air. She could touch any subject and give it truth . . . it was im-
probable that such a poet should ever happen along, but now
that she is with us she is indispensable.[1]

The very next essay in the volume brackets her with W. S. Graham, "the most piquantly original poet now writing in English.
Stevie Smith had rivalled him but at present no one else works so
elfin a touch upon the language." Beneath these airy bubbles of
critical froth there lurk, unexpectedly, some sober critical truths
which call for our attention. Stevie Smith is, after all, no longer
with us, and she is in danger of sinking back, like a character in
one of her poems, beneath the waves of oblivion. The weight of
alleged eccentricity deadens the brightest spirit: as the *Times*
trumpeted at the death of Patrick Kavanagh, "Reputation for
Eccentricity Said to Have Overshadowed Talents as a Writer."
Patrick Kavanagh was a writer who knew and anticipated the
charge of eccentricity:

> O he was eccentric,
> Fol dol the di do,
> He was eccentric
> I tell you.
> ("If Ever You Go to Dublin Town")

Eccentrics are not dangerous, and their value fades with their
passing. As with Kavanagh, Stevie Smith's work has an importance which belies, and is belied by, the image of eccentricity. It
is a paradoxical indication of this importance that Calvin Bedient should, almost unwittingly, sense it for himself without
being able to articulate it. Talk of modern traditions and lines of
development from Larkin towards modernism is misleading:
Stevie Smith presents a peculiar challenge to the reader and
critic. A poet who can so challenge our preconceptions should be
cherished.

1. *Eight Contemporary Poets* (London: Oxford Univ. Press, 1974), 158.

The kind of poet Stevie Smith is begins to emerge from a close look at the *Collected Poems*.[2] She does not develop, in any helpful sense of the word: the first handful of poems announce her concerns as clearly as do the final, posthumous poems. The consistency of technique and craftsmanship is as sure in 1937 as it is in 1969. To say that, though, is to acknowledge the inconsistency too, in that quite often the reader is left wondering whether Stevie Smith knew or cared when she had written a poem not quite true to her Muse. The answer to that sort of nagging doubt is probably that she knew but didn't care all that much. There is a deliberate carelessness in much of her writing which reflects her own rather cavalier attitude both to the world and to poetry; and this carelessness is something the reader has to confront, because it becomes, oddly enough, one of her peculiar strengths (again, the comparison with Kavanagh is instructive). Stevie Smith is sufficiently sure of herself to throw at her audience quite a lot of what, in another context, she calls "balsy nonsense," in the knowledge that, when she has to, she can redeem herself. This process of giving with one hand what she takes away with the other operates through all her work, and it is one which is itself disturbing for readers and critics. We do, after all, like our poets to develop, and to take themselves seriously. But the tendency to see all poets in terms of growth toward maturity, however natural and understandable, is not always illuminating: Keats has suffered because of it, so too has John Clare. Clare in fact provides a useful pointer in the argument, in that he has endured a fate similar to Stevie Smith's at the hands of critics prepared to acknowledge his presence but unwilling to absorb him into their patterns of critical discourse. You will not find Clare getting much of a mention in surveys of the Romantics and Victorians, and this is as much a hint as to his true stature as an indication of his supposedly minor significance. Furthermore, Clare evinces the same sort of inconsistency. Stevie Smith likewise

2. *The Collected Poems of Stevie Smith* (London: Allen Lane, 1975); all further references in this article are to this edition.

stands outside any tradition of the day, and in so doing acts as a comment on what is happening elsewhere; she becomes a touchstone, just as to read Clare is to see him apart from his contemporaries and to see them in a new light.

The comparison with Clare is especially illuminating if we think of Clare's asylum poetry, where his lyricism achieves its fullest and most self-contained flight. Song after song spills out of the notebooks in a profusion that seems to challenge the rigors of critical analysis. It is in the asylum poems that Clare comes closest to Blake. It seems to me significant that Blake, too, can be heard behind and through several of Stevie Smith's poems, and these allusions help to clarify the nature of the critical problem. For, alongside the innocence of Clare, alongside the small cluster of recurrent preoccupations which mark Clare's work and Stevie Smith's, there is the simple directness of Blake as he appears in the *Songs of Innocence and of Experience*. Like Blake, Stevie Smith adorns her margins with her own drawings, which act as comments on her words, sometimes in startling ways: they are, more literally than in Blake's case, marginal drawings, so do not radically alter the poems' status as primarily verbal constructs, but there is sufficient in the comparative point for us to learn from a reading of Blake how to approach Stevie Smith. The other obvious inheritance is the singing voice. Many of Blake's poems can only work when seen as songs to be sung — and there is enough evidence that he thought of them in these terms. When we talk of Blake's songs, then, we do not refer simply to the tone of voice, we refer to a tradition of hymn and song; the same is true of Stevie Smith, who quite often sets her poems to a particular tune, and at poetic readings would sing them in her distinctive, surprising voice. In both cases words on the page, apparently flat and featureless, spring into life, achieve an existence, as song, with song's responsibilities toward clarity and simplicity.

Sooner or later the reader of Stevie Smith's poetry comes up against the problem of simplicity. There are, of course, varieties of simplicity, but it would be true to say that with the *Lyrical*

Ballads Wordsworth sparked off a controversy as to the legitimate uses of simplicity, a controversy which still smolders. Blake's *Songs,* Clare's asylum poems — often entitled "Song" or "Ballad" — were part of that same argument. Neither Blake nor Wordsworth stayed with simplicity: their progression seemed to be a deliberate moving away from its claims and limitations. The critics have moved with them, to a very large extent. It is as though we have lost the ability to be simple, or to acknowledge it and respect it when we see it. Stevie Smith cultivates a particular type of simplicity which has its echoes of Blake especially, but the temptation to move toward greater abstruseness and complexity is always there, and a number of poems can be seen to fail when they succumb in this way. The risks of simplicity, so far as the poet is concerned, are enormous, particularly in an age which distrusts what is simple, which easily perceives when the simple becomes the simplistic. The arch, the knowing, the coy — simplicity attracts such labels. It seems to me that one of Stevie Smith's most important qualities is her determination to persevere within the confines of simplicity, as though at the back of her head all the time is Coleridge's urging of the poet to keep alive in adulthood the simplicity of the child.

Stevie Smith's poems, I have been suggesting, evince preoccupations that are few and insistent — to the point, almost, of repetitiveness. Her poetry, like so many of her characters, teeters on the brink, constantly testing the strength of that "almost." One of her shortest poems runs:

> All things pass
> Love and mankind is grass.

Above the text a couple—apparently middle-aged and bourgeois — embrace on a chaise longue, in a room with patterned wallpaper and frilly curtains. The Biblical portentousness is thereby channeled into something rather startlingly mundane, a reminder of the banality of truth, of the truthfulness of the banal. The poem is no more than embryonic, its rhyme so easily and obviously arrived at, and yet sufficiently noticed for the lines to assume the qualities of an epigram, at once pungent and off-hand. The solidity that attaches itself to this couplet is supported by the way "love and mankind" become a single entity: this reinforces both their interconnectedness (mankind is seen to depend on love) and their fragility (the one will not last any longer than the other). Care has gone into this poem, but it is the kind of care that eschews itself, not wishing to intrude too much.

Stevie Smith's art often depends on what seems to be a carefully contrived carelessness, with respect to life as well as to art, as this neat quatrain "From the Greek" suggests:

> To many men strange fates are given
> Beyond remission or recall
> But the worst fate of all (tra la)
> 's to have no fate at all (tra la).

The seriousness of the first two lines is answered by the hardheaded wryness of the last two: the rhythmic change of gear and the mindless "tra la's" are devices which allow the poet to slip out from the intractabilities of the initial proposition. Even a poem as slight as this reminds us that for Stevie Smith life is a matter of pain, of lost love, of desperation — and these things urge humor for their control. It is as though she engages us in the halting gait of a danse macabre where love and death and solitude hold hands; the music she dances to is generally quiet, offbeat — or, if it is noisy, the din rings slightly hollow. One of her poems celebrates Miss Pauncefort who "sang at the top of her voice . . . And nobody knew what she sang about" (which did not stop her singing in her manic way). The Muse for Stevie Smith tends to be quiet, even timid. "Dear Muse" hints at the relationship:

> Dear Muse, the happy hours we have spent together.
> I love you so much in wet or fine weather.

I only wish sometimes you would speak louder,
But perhaps you will do so when you are prouder.
I often think that this will be the next instant,
Meanwhile I am your most obliging confidante.

What here is friendly, muted, happy is elsewhere seen as frightening in its tenuousness:

Who is this that howls and mutters?
It is the Muse, each word she utters
Is thrown against a shuttered door
And very soon she'll speak no more.

Cry louder, Muse, make much more noise
The world is full of rattling toys
I thought she'd say, Why should I then?
I have spoke low to better men
But oh she did not speak at all but went away
And now I search for her by night and day . . .

This relationship between Muse and poet is central to her vision, and to how Stevie Smith sees herself as a poet: it helps to explain her gait, her step at once firm and tentative.

"On the Death of a German Philosopher" is of interest in this connection, in that the poem manages to dismiss him even whilst reclaiming him (and vice versa). Stevie Smith sets little store by philosophical claptrap, and yet this epitaph appears to draw us all within its helpless confines. It is another poem that is all but thrown away, and we are left to admire the sleight of hand, the summation and the discardment. The tight, short lines deceive us, so that we are not prepared for that final switch, in the last line, to us all, to our own floundering.

He wrote *The I and the It*
He wrote *The It and the Me*
He died at Marienbad
And now we are all at sea.

The rhyme, and its colloquial rightness, is a stamp of Stevie Smith's authority. Being at sea—something to which she alludes frequently — necessitates a constant search for bearings. Stevie Smith finds her bearings in rhyme, and it is significant that poems which dispense with rhyme dribble away into quaintness and inconsequentiality.

There is clearly a slightness about the poems I have mentioned so far, and it is important to acknowledge this. Stevie Smith's immersion in Blake helps her here in that it enables her to explore beyond the limits of such insistent simplicities. In some poems, the Blakean echoes are obviously deliberate, and the paradox is that such echoes point up the distance between Blake's world of Innocence and Stevie Smith's world of Experience. In "Heber" Stevie Smith takes up the implicit challenge of Blake's "Chimney sweeper" in *Songs of Innocence,* which has worried readers with its apparently naïve and simplistic morality ("Though the morning was cold, Tom was happy and warm; So if all do their duty they need not fear harm").

> I love little Heber
> His coat is so warm
> And if I don't speak to him
> He'll do me no harm
> But sit by my window
> And stare in the street
> And pull up a hassock for the comfort of his feet.

(In passing, in view of the connections with Clare as well as Blake, it is worth noting that "I Am," which picks up Clare's existential cry and turns it upside down, refers to the same conventional morality that sparks off this poem: these lines could almost be by Blake:

> Then a priest came and told him if he was good
> And thought as he ought and did as he should
> He should be saved by the Lamb's fresh blood.)

Stevie Smith has complicated the Blakean rhyme by making the
conditional a rather daunting negative which in its turn chills
the deceptive warmth of that coat and therefore of this relationship, this love. The indeterminate nature of Heber — hovering
between the human and the animal — add to the sense of distance between the two of them. The surprisingly lengthened final line of the stanza underlines the deliberate, teasing action
which is solely self-centered, and by no means an indication of
reciprocated affection: the implicit comfort of the relationship is
uncomfortably threatened. The second stanza reminds us of the
closeness of Blake's inspiration to conventional religious hym-
nody; and if we catch, albeit momentarily, the presence of a pro-
tecting God who will always "stay by my side," then that makes
all the more effective the disillusionment attendant on such final
dependence (and more sinister the faint echoes of "Away in a
manager").

> I love little Heber
> His eyes are so wide
> And if I don't speak to him
> He'll stay by my side.
> But oh in this silence
> I find but suspense:
> I must speak have spoken have driven him hence.

(Clare's "Secret Love," with its similar emphasis on a madden-
ingly silenced love, springs to mind as an obvious analogue.) The
silence of an unreciprocated relationship is intolerable; but to
speak is to destroy it, and that is worse. Stevie Smith's art thrives
on the tensions that arise when emotion is invested without return, on this cruel paradox whereby the necessity of silence is
outweighed by the compelling necessity of speech. "The Word"
— a later poem — crystalizes this contradiction:

> My heart leaps up with streams of joy,
> My lips tell of drouth;

> Why should my heart be full of joy
> And not my mouth?
>
> I fear the Word, to speak or write it down,
> I fear all that is brought to birth and born;
> This fear has turned my joy into a frown.

Stevie Smith is making a connection between her dramatized experience and her role as poet, and in doing this she is going beyond Blake, who rarely, even in the dourest Songs of Experience, suggests that the agonized and terrified consciousness is his. That is the difference between his poem "Little Boy Lost" and Stevie Smith's of the same name:

> The wood was rather old and dark
> The witch was very ugly
> And if it hadn't been for father
> Walking there so smugly
> I never should have followed
> The beckoning of her finger . . .

It might seem that Stevie Smith is in danger of diluting the strength of what she has inherited from Blake; the prominent adverbs dissipate rather than concentrate intensity: "rather old," "very ugly," "I really cannot see." But this is the way of the poem:

> It's not a bad place in a way
> But I lost the way
> Last Tuesday
> Did I love father, mother, home?
> Not very much; but now they're gone
> I think of them with kindly toleration
> Bred inevitably of separation.
> Really if I could find some food
> I should be happy enough in this wood . . .

Such qualifications are crucial to the poem's tone, and make the earlier poeticized image of the sun seem particularly inappropriate:

> I lift my hand but it never reaches
> To where the breezes toss
> The sun-kissed leaves above.

The poem does not work because ultimately the little boy lost is transparently a surrogate of a poet without bearings. Much more successful is "Little Boy Sick," where the Blakean idiom is recreated, and at the same time the dramatized utterance retains its integrity. The little lamb of Innocence has become a mangy tiger, his former glory departed utterly. Here is something of Stevie Smith's surprising virtuosity — surprising in that she would be the first to disclaim virtuosity:

> I am not God's little lamb
> I am God's sick tiger,
> And I prowl about at night
> And what most I love I bite,
> And upon the jungle grass I slink,
> Snuff the aroma of my mental stink,
> Taste the salt tang of tears upon the brink
> Of my uncomfortable muzzle.
> My tail my beautiful, my lovely tail,
> Is warped.
> My stripes are matted and my coat once sleek
> Hangs rough and undistinguished on my bones.
> O God I was so beautiful when I was well.
> My heart, my lungs, my sinews and my reins
> Consumed a solitary ecstasy.
> And light and pride informed each artery.
> Then I a temple, now a charnal house.
> Then I a high hozannah, now a dirge.
> Then I a recompense of God's endeavour,

Now a reproach and earnest of lost toil.
Consider, Lord, a tiger's melancholy
And heed a minished tiger's muted moan,
For thou art sleek and shining bright
And I am weary.
Thy countenance is full of light
And mine is dreary.

The range of voices here is wide, but never so much so that the
poem gets out of control: we are constantly brought back to the
tautness of Blake's "Tyger," its impressed syntax. At the epicen-
ter of the poem lies the audacious line "O God I was so beautiful
when I was well" which echoes, if anything, the stark cry in a
Brecht/Weill song, "Surabaya Johnny, my God, and I love you
so," and has the same chokingly dramatic effect: typically the
cry to God is both colloquial blasphemy and desperate appeal.
Once again, Blake's world of experience is the one which has its
special meaning for Stevie Smith; it is characteristic of her deep-
seated pessimism that she should choose the only optimistic
poem in Blake's canon of Experience as a jumping-off point for
an exploration of her own desolation.

In many respects, Stevie Smith shares Blake's vision, when it
comes to a hatred of cant and suppression. For all her fear of emotion and its deceptions, she attacks bland indifference whenever
she sees it. In "Oh, if only . . . " the "intellectual Englishman"
confronts his rival, in bed with the "Englishwoman Blah." If the
form the poem takes (long loping unrhymed lines) is uncharac-
teristic, the situation is typical. The dried-up intellect cannot
cope: at least the man of action, the soldier Thomas—even if he
is inarticulate—has action on his side, so that his "Go to hell"
has a force the intellectual's lacks. The intellectual marvels at the
woman's smugness, at "The satisfaction, the noble-animal dignity, the imperial carelessness!" As he creeps away at the end of
the poem, the poet comments, "Oh, if he could only experience
emotional extravagance!" In this context, then, carelessness and
extravagance are virtues: it is almost a twentieth-century version of *The Visions of the Daughters of Albion,* in that the possessive

lover is no better (is worse in fact) than the seducer. We can understand why Stevie Smith admires "The Ambassador": "in the underworld he rides carelessly," which seems to enable him to soar free of the earth altogether— "Sometimes he rises into the air and flies silently." One of Stevie Smith's most famous poems, "Pad, Pad," earns its resonance from this kind of association: the carefree rhythms of the first part of the poem underline the true boldness of emotion of the past:

> I always remember your beautiful flowers
> And the beautiful kimono you wore
> When you sat on the couch
> With that tigerish crouch
> And told me you loved me no more.
>
> What I cannot remember is how I felt when you were unkind
> All I know is, if you were unkind now I should not mind.
> Ah me, the power to feel exaggerated, angry and sad
> They years have taken from me. Softly I go now, pad, pad.

An earlier poem puts the case for truthfulness to feeling with great spareness and force: this is one of the few poems where Stevie Smith does not need the prop of rhyme, so directly aimed is her shaft.

> I have no respect for you
> For you would not tell the truth about your grief
> But laughed at it
> When the first pang was past
> And made it a thing of nothing.
> You said
> That what had been
> Had never been
> That what was
> Was not:
> You have a light mind
> And a coward's soul.
>
> ("No Respect")

This poem can only work if we regard the poet's respect as something worth having, if in other words we respect the poet. Stevie Smith gains our respect because she can use humor and still tell the truth: she will give emotion its due weight. Just how painful a process this is emerges in one of her most haunting "confessional" poems, "Dirge":

> From a friend's friend I taste friendship,
> From a friend's friend love,
> My spirit in confusion,
> Long years I strove,
> But now I know that never
> Nearer I shall move,
> Than a friend's friend to friendship,
> To love than a friend's love.
>
> Into the dark night
> Resignedly I go,
> I am not so afraid of the dark night
> As the friends I do not know,
> I do not fear the night above,
> As I fear the friends below.

Emotional truth, then, does not come easily, and Stevie Smith can talk about respect (that rather formal word which can indicate the most deep-seated of relationships) because she is prepared to respect the feelings of others. And of course this element of respect, of our respect as readers, is only valid in poetry where the poet's presence is central; we rely on a specific type of integrity (it is not an easy autobiographical relationship) and can do so because we know the poet's presence and can recognize the voice's morality:

> You have a light mind
> And a coward's soul.

To such an indictment there is no purely aesthetic response: to ram the point home Stevie Smith has denied herself "poetic" devices. Hers is poetry of statement with a vengeance, all the more telling when set off against the poet's dreamworld in which such directness can be avoided:

> In my dreams I am always saying goodbye and riding away,
> Whither and why I know not nor do I care.
> And the parting is sweet and the parting over is sweeter,
> And sweetest of all is the night and the rushing air.
>
> In my dreams they are always waving their hands and
>   saying goodbye,
> And they give me the stirrup cup and I smile as I drink,
> I am glad the journey is set, I am glad I am going,
> I am glad, I am glad, that my friends don't know what I think.
> ("In My Dreams")

Scrupulosity is the hallmark of another poem, "To the Tune of the Coventry Carol," in which typically English compromise is condemned as the worst evil. The poem's force depends on its curiously carefree structure and movement; the tight form allows a freedom and a naturalness, so that the final line (with its semi-jocular feminine rhyme) is in effect thrown away. This is not rhyme that rounds on the poem epigrammatically, it is a turning away, a liberation.

> The nearly right
> And yet not quite
> In love is wholly evil
> And every heart
> That loves in part
> Is mortgaged to the devil.
>
> I loved or thought
> I loved in sort
> Was this to love akin

> To take the best
> And leave the rest
> And let the devil in?
>
> O lovers true
> And others too
> Whose best is only better
> Take my advice
> Shun compromise
> Forget him and forget her.

The very notion of carelessness is canvassed in a poem which examines the possible meanings of the word "Pretty" — "Why is the word pretty so underrated?" The word comes to mean practically anything, it encompasses the savageries as well as the beauties of nature: what seems essentially to matter is the prodigality of nature.

> All this looks easy but really it is extraordinary
> Well, it is extraordinary to be so pretty.
>
> And it is careless, and that is always pretty
> This field, this owl, this pike, this pool are careless,
> As Nature is always careless and indifferent
> Who sees, who steps, means nothing, and this is pretty.
>
> So a person can come along like a thief — pretty! —
> Stealing a look, pinching the sound and feel,
> Lick the icicle broken from the bank
> And still say nothing at all, only cry pretty.
>
> Cry pretty, pretty, pretty and you'll be able
> Very soon not even to cry pretty
> And so be delivered entirely from humanity
> This is prettiest of all, it is very pretty.
>
> ("Pretty")

A hackneyed word suddenly loses its initial pallid meaning; a word particularly of childhood (the illustration shows a child with a limp-looking cat on her lap) has survived to become something sinister and adult. Nature's carelessness — so prized in this poem — is reflected in the dominating aesthetic of carelessness: Stevie Smith seems to have won the secret Patrick Kavanagh won, of knowing "how not to care." But it is won at a price, we might feel. If we are unsettled by this poem, it might well be because of its move toward cynicism and heartlessness. And yet, such heartlessness helps to ease her away from a simplistic sweetness. "Pretty" seems to me to present one of the central problems for Stevie Smith, and her readers: how can she be direct and uncompromising, without being totally negative; how can the aesthetic carelessness unite convincingly with an emotional carelessness that is not simply stupid?

Several dramatic poems concern the griefs of others. Stevie Smith has a number of ballads which in their spareness echo the asperities of Auden's "Victor" and "Miss Gee": the heartlessness operates here, too. Mrs. Simpkins, for example, gets a raw deal. She attends spiritualist sessions where she is assured death is not the end; and she goes home to tell her husband, who is less than overjoyed to hear he'll not after all get away from his relatives, or even his wife, after death.

> "It's the truth" Mrs. Simpkins affirmed, "there is no separation
> There's a great reunion coming for which this life's but a
>   preparation."

Stevie Smith's sympathies are with the husband, and Mrs. Simpkins is left suspended at the end of the poem:

> This worked him to such a pitch that he shot himself through
>   the head
> And now she has to polish the floors of Westminster County hall
>   for her daily bread.
>   ("Mrs. Simpkins")

The McGonagallesque rhythm and rhyme carry Mrs. Simpkins into the absurd.

But we could argue that Stevie Smith can be hard on others because she is hard on herself. The dangers of unhealthy introspection are acknowledged repeatedly, as in "Analysand":

> All thoughts that are turned inward to their source
> Bring one to self-hatred and remorse
> The punishment is suicide of course.
>
> But is it surprising Reader do you think?
> Would you expect to find him in the pink
> Who's solely occupied with his own mental stink?

This fastidiousness saves her from herself time and again: it is a fastidiousness which refuses agonized emotional indulgence whilst allowing the suffering of "Appetite":

> Let me know
> Let me know
> Let me go
> Let me go
> Let me have him
> Let me have him
> How I love him
> How I love him.

The voice in this poem cries out to be heard, like the obsession that drives, for example, poor Harold to his final leap over the cliff ("It was a brave thing to do"). It also acts as a corrective to the quaintness, the whiff of Gothicism that can be sniffed in some of the poems. Any poet who courts death so studiously is liable to fall foul of her intentions, to end up with all the trappings but little of the emotional substance: the fate of the eighteenth-century "graveyard school" should act as a constant warning to poets obsessed with death. "Study to Deserve Death" fails because of its reliance on pious cliché—

> Study to deserve Death they only may
> Who fought well upon their earthly day,
> Who never sheathed their swords or ran away —

but the idea behind the poem matters enormously. Stevie Smith sees life as preparation for death in a sense quite different from that understood by Mrs. Simpkins. To deserve death means to understand its significance, its horror, and its release.

An early poem "Night-time in the Cemetery" is one of her most moving poems because it acknowledges the bitterness of death even as it recognizes the affinity. Here Stevie Smith strives to deserve the death she is to court more stoically elsewhere. It is not fanciful to hear Blake and Clare behind this poem, even Emily Dickinson; yet at the very core is the unmistakable figure, the Stevie Smith whose colloquial twang explains the Clare-like insistence on peculiarity and strangeness (see Clare's "I am" — "Strange, nay, rather stranger than the rest"):

> The funeral paths are hung with snow
> About the graves the mourners go
> To think of those who lie below.
> The churchyard pales are black against the night
> And snow hung here seems doubly white.
> I have a horror of this place
> A horror of each moonlit mourner's face
> These people are not familiar
> But strange and stranger than strange peculiar
> They have that look of a cheese do you know sour-sweet
> You can smell their feet.
> Yet must I tread
> About my dead
> And guess the forms within the grave
> And hear the clank of jowl on jowl
> Where low lie kin no love could save.
> Yet stand I by my grave as they by theirs. Oh bitter Death
> That brought their love and mine unto a coffin's breadth.

This poem is a triumph of Stevie Smith's idiosyncratic art, and we learn not to be surprised by the fact that it comes so early in the canon: she returns to this world repeatedly, to weave variations of the subtlest and most lyrical kind on the theme of death and oblivion. She knows that the theme is inexhaustible, and that it is necessary, however hard that acknowledgment, when it would be so much easier, as in her dreams, to run away from it all.

The reader of Stevie Smith finds himself making a long list of the memorable poems: there are far more poems announcing their authority than I have been able to hint at. It is ironic that a poet so concerned with scrupulosity, with the quietness of the Muse's voice, should be so fecund. She herself worries at this a lot, often referring to the parable of the talents. In the last resort her claim on posterity rests on this extraordinary combination of the minimal and the generous. In one sense, her work is a burden to her, something she lands herself with:

> I can call up old ghosts, and they will come,
> But my art limps, — I cannot send them home.
>
> ("Old Ghosts")

But she accepts the limp, learns to live with the ghosts that haunt her, until she is able to celebrate them. Her poems on death, on the myth of Persephone, on Venus when young, — these are, astonishingly, amongst the most positive things she does. Her final poem, "Come Death," seems to be the distillation of her life's work:

> I feel ill, What can the matter be?
> I'd ask God to have pity on me,
> But I turn to the one I know, and say:
> Come, Death, and carry me away.
>
> Ah me, sweet Death, you are the only god
> Who comes as a servant when he is called, you know,
> Listen then to this sound I make, it is sharp,
> Come Death. Do not be slow.

But in case we remember only the sweetness of death, rather than its sharpness, it is salutary to read, alongside this, her poem "Voice from the Tomb (Nightmare, after Reading The Parable of the Talents)." Only a true and significant poet could capture this nightmare with such pungency, and proceed to counter it. That, ultimately, is why Stevie Smith matters.

> Here lies a poet who would not write
> His soul runs screaming through the night
> Oh give me paper, give me pen,
> And I will very soon begin.
>
> Poor Soul, keep silent; in Death's clime
> There's no pen, paper, notion,
> And no Time.

1979

*

Stevie Smith
The Art of Sinking in Poetry

CHRISTOPHER RICKS

Fausse-naïve: an odd turn, but Philip Larkin[1] devised it as a route into the world of Stevie Smith. All its quirks are right for this truly quirky poet: its feminizing, its Anglo-French, and its paradox. For the first question to ask about the poems of Stevie Smith is, can she possibly be as ingenuous as she sounds? An ingénue is of interest only if you can't be entirely sure. A few critics raise the question and show that it need not be nailed down. If critics "portray her often as a naïve writer," says Michael Schmidt, "this reveals the success with which she projected the mock-innocence of her public image."[2] But her writing depends upon its being always in question to what degree her innocence *is* mock-innocence. She disliked "the false-simple" (which she associated with Nazism) as much as she liked "the childish delight in a daily use of colour and form, the naïveté that has in it something of innocence."[3] Not that innocence is a simple thing. In the words of "The Last Turn of the Screw": "Some children

1. "Frivolous and Vulnerable," *New Statesman,* 28 Sept. 1962, 416; reprinted in *Required Writing* (London: Faber, 1983), 153.
2. *An Introduction to Fifty Modern British Poets* (London: Pan Books, 1979), 200.
3. *The Holiday* (London: Chapman and Hall, 1949; London: Virago, 1979), 143 – 44. *Over the Frontier* (London: Cape, 1938; London: Virago, 1980), 271.

are born innocent, some achieve it." And some have it thrust upon them? In her novel *The Holiday,* she permitted herself a risqué joke by allusion to a low paper, yet she did so in schoolgirl French: As the sunlight saturates my flesh and bones I feel I should like it to go on for a long time (comme disait Ingenuous Isabel dans le Pink 'Un d'autrefois)."[4] To speak in this way of Ingenuous Isabel must be to leave the question of Ingenuous Stevie or Disingenuous Stevie teasingly unresolved.

When she deprecated the political animus of *Murder in the Cathedral,* she went for an unexpected double charge that it was both childish and disingenuous:

> This does not seem a constructive political opinion, it seems rather childish, as if he thought men did not sometimes have to govern, as if he thought that by the act of governing they became at once not men but monsters. It is a disingenuous and not uncommon thought, it is one aspect of the arrogance of art and the arrogance of highmindedness divorced from power, it is something one should not put up with.[5]

The word "disingenuous" turns up in "Private Means Is Dead," an early poem partly about the language's being eager to doff its civilian clothes and don its uniform. "Major Portion/Is a disingenuous person." Others in this monstrous regiment of men are Private Means; Major Operation; the Generals Collapse, Debility, Panic, and Uproar; and a disguised figure (unseen but not unheard), "The crux and Colonel/Of the whole matter." Yet the crux and kernel of the poem must be acknowledged, namely the Shakespearean allusion:

> Captive Good, attending Captain Ill
> Can tell us quite a lot about the Captain, if he will.

4. *Holiday,* 149.
5. "History or Poetic Drama?" in *T. S. Eliot: A Symposium for His Seventieth Birthday,* ed. Neville Braybrooke (London: Hart-Davis, 1958), reprinted in *Me Again* (London: Virago Press, 1981), 148.

For Shakespeare's Sonnet 66 was never far from her thoughts: "Tyr'd with all these for restfull death I cry." Many of her best poems cry for restful death: "Come Death" (the early poem, and also her very last, which used the title again), "Tender Only to One," "The Bottle of Aspirins," "The Hostage," "My Heart Goes Out," "Thoughts about the Person from Porlock," and "Why Do I Think of Death as a Friend?" In *The Holiday* there is a telling moment: "And I smile at Basil and I say: Tired of all these, for restful death I cry, as to behold desert a beggar born."[6]

> And simple-Truth miscalde Simplicitie,
> And captive-good attending Captaine ill.

Miscalled simplicity? She was not simple-minded, and speaking to her friend Kay Dick, she declined to be assimilated to Phèdre: "She's much simpler than I am . . . I'm straightforward but I'm not simple."[7] As she put it in "Phèdre":

> Yes, I should like poor honourable simple sweet prim Phèdre
> To be happy. One would have to be pretty simple
> To be happy with a prig like Hippolytus,
> But she was simple.

Still, whether or not this was the simple biographical truth, it is not the truth that the poems promulgate.

MAGNA EST VERITAS

> With my looks I am bound to look simple or fast I would rather
>   look simple
> So I wear a tall hat on the back of my head that is rather a
>   temple
> And I walk rather queerly and comb my long hair
> And people say, Don't bother about her.

6. *Holiday,* 17.
7. *Ivy and Stevie* (London: Duckworth, 1971), 49.

So in my time I have picked up a good many facts,
Rather more than the people do who wear smart hats
And I do not deceive because I am rather simple too
And although I collect facts I do not always know what they
    amount to.
I regard them as a contribution to almighty Truth, magna est
    veritas et praevalebit,
Agreeing with that Latin writer, Great is Truth and will prevail
    in a bit.

Simple truth, or affection? The odd gait of the lines ("And I walk
rather queerly"); the queer freedom suddenly to lop their lollop-
ing, so that the lines can lope and pace; the off-rhyming, offhand
but also a bit off its head; the straight gaze and straight face
which can then move from one kind of inspired inane rhyming
("too" with "to") into another kind: "et praevalebit" with "and
will prevail in a bit": these constitute the art of a poem which
will not let on how artless or artful it is being.

Stevie Smith once produced an anthology of children's verse,
The Batsford Book of Children's Verse (1970), which was sold in
America without "children" in the title. But then who but she
would have prefaced such a collection by giving these lines by
Shelley as just the thing for children?

> His big tears, for he wept well,
> Turned to mill-stones as they fell;
>
> And the little children, who
> Round his feet played to and fro,
> Thinking every tear a gem
> Had their brains knocked out by them.

None of the things that come together in her poems is in itself
unusual, but the combination is unique. The accents are those of
a child; yet the poems are continually allusive, alive with literary
echoes as no child's utterance is. The accents are those of a child,
and at the same time of a patient instructor of a child. The poems

sound like child's-play, but are inimitable. In their memories of nursery rhyme and of fairy tale, in their lisping and lilting, they are a child's eye view; yet children don't write poems which matter except as that diminished thing, poems-by-children. Helen Vendler pointed out a paradox:

> All poetry deserving of the name has been written by people who have passed through puberty. On the other hand, there are some aspects of poetry — notably, originality of perception and spontaneity of language — which appear frequently in the speech and writing of children, but which are so dishearteningly killed off by life and schooling that a way with words is one of the rarest of adult talents.[8]

This is a paradox which Stevie Smith's poems not only embody but also attend to, albeit cryptically.

WHAT IS SHE WRITING? PERHAPS IT WILL BE GOOD

What is she writing? Perhaps it will be good,
The young girl laughs: "I am in love."
But the older girl is serious: "Not now, perhaps later."
Still the young girl teases: "What's the matter?
To lose everything! A waste of time!"
But now the older one is quite silent,
Writing, writing, and perhaps it will be good.
Really neither girl is a fool.

When the child prodigy Minou Drouet burst upon French life with her poems, Jean Cocteau stood firm. "All eight-year-olds have genius — except Minou Drouet." Yet really neither girl is a fool. Stevie Smith played the fool; and she held this high-spirited modesty in tension with a higher spirit.

Behind her simplest work is a very unsimple tradition: *The Praise of Folly.* The account of Erasmus's book given by William

8. *New York Review of Books,* 24 Nov. 1977.

Empson, in *The Structure of Complex Words,* suits Stevie Smith and her proclivity to use the word "fool" widely and discriminatingly. "We could indeed say," says Empson, "that the simpleton is innocent and natural; this sums up most of the conception."[9] Stevie Smith was a natural. "Simpletons, children, madmen of various sorts, saints": these are the types who throng forward with a claim to Erasmus's invaluable folly, and they are the types who populate her poems. One novelty here is that the poet, the Fool, is a woman. After all, the Fool is most often a man. Stevie Smith is still further seen as Fool (as well as minstrel) in her extraordinarily funny account, all piercing simplicity (in Kay Dick's *Ivy and Stevie*[10]), of her audience with the Queen in Buckingham Palace, when she received the Queen's Gold Medal for poetry in 1969.

Among her many subjects, Stevie Smith had two great ones, children and death. Her excellent perturbed critiques of Christianity — doubly perturbed in that, as she said, she was always in danger of falling into belief[11] — are essentially death-poems: they believe eternal life to be a threat and not a promise, and not only when it takes the form of eternal torment.

Yet children and death sit oddly together. The usual thing is to say that children cannot imagine death. Stevie Smith insists that she for one could and did. At the age of about eight, she realized that if life were more than she could bear, she could decide not to bear it. "Life lay in our hands."[12] No doubt she was precocious, but her art has the disturbing power to suggest that in this matter too we sentimentalize children. They have intimations of mortality; they should be educated, she says, explicitly in the feasibility and — on occasion — propriety of suicide. Her

9. *The Structure of Complex Words* (London: Chatto and Windus, 1951), 106–7.

10. *Ivy,* 51–52.

11. "The Necessity of Not Believing," *Gemini* 2, no. 1 (1958): 19–32.

12. Preface to *The Batsford Book of Children's Verse* (London: Batsford, 1970). Also *Novel on Yellow Paper* (London: Cape, 1936; Harmondsworth: Penguin, 1951), 135–37.

anthology of children's verse, or rather of verse for children, offers not only Spenser's Despair and Shakespeare's "Fear no more
the heat of the sun," but also the dark old consolation that it is
better to be dead than alive, best of all never to have been born.
"From *Oedipus at Colonus* (Sophocles)":

> *Chorus:*   Not to be born at all
>   Is best, far best that can befall,
>   Next best, when born, with least delay
>   To trace the backward way.

A riddling consolation. Perhaps it is not that children are more
like adults than is generally assumed in that both can imagine
death, but in that neither can. (Though it is the adult who can
imagine the unimaginability of death.) *Imagination Dead Imagine* intones the greatest of these modern writers who are grateful,
as Stevie Smith was, to believe that there is no such thing as eternal life. When Samuel Beckett, in *Murphy,* refers darkly to "the
next best thing to never being born," we know where we are. As
we do when Stevie Smith issues a simple remonstrance: "There
are some human beings who do not wish for eternal life."[13]
    The crucial critical question is the same for her as for Beckett.
Since each subscribes to the belief that life is not simply a good
thing or death simply a bad thing, what sort of life should there
be in their words? The young Beckett could praise the words of
James Joyce because "they are alive," they are not "abstracted to
death."[14] But Beckett became a great writer once he realized that
it does not make sense to use the word "life" approvingly of
words, and "death" disapprovingly, if you do not yourself happily approve of life and disapprove of death. The very words must
incarnate the acknowledgment, a relationship of life to death, as
they did when Robert Lowell fashioned wording glad to be sud-

---

13. With a sketch reproduced in *New Directions,* nos. 7 – 8 and 10 – 11
(1975): 19.
    14. *Our Exagmination Round His Factification . . .* (Paris: Shakespeare and
Co., 1929, 15 – 16.

denly cut short: "All's well that ends." Less curt, more sidling, Stevie Smith works towards the same end: "But all good things come to an end, and the same goes for all bad things."[15] Death is the nothing that supremely ends all bad things, and her language will bring a spectral life to what is usually a moribund turn of phrase:

> When I was talking to Harley at the Ministry one day about my poems, he said, I am rather disturbed about this death feeling in your poems.
> Oh, I said, that is nothing, that death feeling, it is absolutely nothing.[16]

For "that death feeling" is not only one's feelings about death, but also there being no feeling once dead, and "absolutely nothing" is not only a social soothing but "the vision of *positive* annihilation" (in the words of Beckett).[17] Absolutely, that is what death is: nothing. "Be absolute for death," in the words of the Duke in *Measure for Measure*. "Why do I think of death as a friend?": there is no question about the answer.

So Stevie Smith, like Beckett, uses clichés; they are phrases which are dead but won't lie down. From *The Holiday:*

> I said to my cousin on another occasion when we had gone horseback riding together: Do you like Death?
> Caz said: He is nothing to write home about.[18]

Beckett is a writer who did wonders with this cliché, nothing to write home about: see his story, *The End.*

Again like Beckett, she uses literary allusions to catch a paradox of life and death, of life in death or death in life.

15. *Novel on Yellow,* 155.
16. *Holiday,* 62.
17. To Joseph Hone, in Deirdre Bair, *Samuel Beckett* (New York: Harcourt Brace Jovanovich, 1978), 254.
18. *Holiday,* 151.

Tennyson: Deep as first love, and wild with all regret;
O Death in Life, the days that are no more.

("Tears, Idle Tears")

Beckett: "O Death in Life," vociferated Belacqua, "the days that are no more."[19]

Stevie Smith: I think of my poems as my kiddo, and no doubt but Tennyson felt that way too, "Deep as first love and wild with all regret, Oh death in Life the days that are no more."[20]

THE DEATH SENTENCE

Cold as No Plea,
Yet wild with all negation,
Weeping I come
To my heart's destination,
To my last bed
Between th'unhallowed boards —
The Law allows it
And the Court awards.

For all its articulations, "The Death Sentence" is one sentence, and it is more merciful than the poem called "The Commuted Sentence," next in the *Collected Poems,* which opens:

Shut me not alive away
From the light of every day
Hang me rather by the neck to die
Against a morning sky.

"The Death Sentence" begins in Tennyson, and in the eerie death in life of a phrase torn from its original life; it echoes her own very short "Quand on n'a pas ce que l'on aime, il faut aimer ce que l'on a—":

19. "Love and Lethe," in *More Pricks Than Kicks* (New York: Grove, 1972), 96.
20. *Novel on Yellow,* 23.

Cold as no love, and wild with all negation —
Oh Death in Life, the lack of animation.

And it ends in Shakespeare, in Portia's acquiescence in the law's severity of justice. (Stevie Smith wrote in *The Holiday*, "And I thought that Shakespeare had caught in a phrase the cruelty and blindness of the world and of history, 'the law allows it, and the court awards.' ")[21] Her lineation in the poem breaks the backs of both the Tennyson and the Shakespeare lines and then does not put them out of their misery. Such ways with words are a counterpart to the explicit death in life in a characteristic poem, "Under Wrong Trees":

Under wrong trees
Walked the zombies

Yet her most distinctive ways are with rhythm and rhyme. From her early "Death Came to Me":

For underneath the superscription lurked I knew
With pulse quickening and the blood thickening
For fear in every vein the deadly strychnine.

The sequence "quickening," "thickening," "strychnine," makes for a killing rhyme, like a killing joke, especially given what it is to quicken. Such rhyming is both youthful and deathwards, and it illuminates a paradox which she herself acknowledged: "I'm astonished the young like my poems. They're rather melancholy on the whole . . . I say to them, I can't see what you see in them, because on the whole they're a bit deathwards in their wish."[22] But poems which are deathwards in their wish must be deathwards in their words, too, even if they also need to be suf-

21. *Holiday*, 130.
22. *Ivy*, 48.

ficiently alive for their death wish to impinge. "Oh Death in Life, the lack of animation."

In rhythm and rhyme, she found her deathwards animation most vividly and memorially. "A Dream of Comparison," which is about a conversation between Eve and Mary, turning on whether death is unimaginable and undesirable, ends like this:

> They walked by the estuary,
> Eve and the Virgin Mary,
> And they talked until nightfall,
> But the difference between them was radical.

The rhymes poleax the poles of the argument. These are "Simpsonian rhymes," to use the term wielded by C. S. Lewis (after the scholar who first diagnosed the disease). In his *English Literature in the Sixteenth Century,* Lewis is eloquent about these extraordinary rhymes—extraordinary in that we can't now see how it was that good and even great poets were happy to rhyme, for instance, "on the second syllable of a disyllabic word where metre forbids that syllable to carry the stress."[23] Here, however, is Stevie Smith's achievement, since she apprehended that this "metrical phenomenon distressing to the modern ear" may be perfect for distress signals. It is also a deadly or deathly thing to do, and a poet who was happy about death would be happy sometimes to rhyme so. "The Murderer" ends:

> She was not like other girls—rather diffident,
> And that is how we had an accident.

What a diffident accident a rhyme may be—and no less lethal for that. A rhyme might be expected to be a coupling which will rise as an arch; in her poems, it is a couple which leaves all in rubble—itself a rhyme to which she turned and turned:

---

23. *English Literature in the Sixteenth Century* (Oxford: Clarendon, 1954), 478–79.

Thus spake the awful aging couple
Whose heart the years had turned to rubble.

> ("Advice to Young Children")

They were a precious couple,
And let the people feed on straw and rubble.

> ("Après la Politique, la Haine des Bourbons")

Banausic, he called them banausic,
A villainous banausic couple.
He turned to blow on his love for his father
And found it rubble.

> ("Easy")

Such rhyming reaches its high point in the nadir of a dyslectic rhyme like this, about a bust of mother:

> Upon its plinth
> It beholds the zenith
> Of my success on the pianoforte.

This is from a poem called "The Virtuoso"; it is itself a piece of virtuosity in *The Art of Sinking in Poetry.*

The third Class remains, of the *Diminishing* Figures: And first, The ANTICLIMAX, where the second Line drops quite short of the first, than which nothing creates greater Surprize.

At other times this Figure operates in a larger Extent; and when the gentle Reader is in Expectation of some great Image, he either finds it surprizingly *imperfect,* or is presented with something very *low,* or quite *ridiculous.* A Surprize resembling that of a curious Person in a Cabinet of Antique Statues, who beholds on the Pedestal the Names of *Homer,* or *Cato;* but looking up, finds *Homer* without a Head, and nothing to be seen of *Cato* but his privy Member.

> (ch. xi)

Poetry is tempted to say, lo and behold. The art of sinking in poetry presents "something very *low*" to a reader "who beholds on
the Pedestal the Names of *Homer,* or of *Cato.*"

> Upon its plinth
> It beholds the zenith
> Of my success on the pianoforte.

Much of this classic Augustan essay in mock-criticism (1727)
is germane to Stevie Smith. She cultivated the art of sinking, the
stone of bathos falling through the waters of pathos.

> The Taste of the *Bathos* is implanted by Nature itself in the Soul
> of Man; 'till perverted by Custom or Example he is taught, or
> rather compell'd, to relish the *Sublime.* Accordingly, we see the
> unprejudiced Minds of Children delight only in such Produc-
> tions, and in such Images, as our true modern Writers set before
> them. I have observ'd how fast the general Taste is returning to
> this first Simplicity and Innocence.
>
> (ch. ii)

There is the Anticlimax. There is the Infantine: "This is when a
Poet grows so very simple, as to think and talk like a Child."
There is the Inanity, or Nothingness. There is the Mixture of
Figures:

> Its principal Beauty is when it gives an Idea just opposite to what
> it seem'd meant to describe. Thus an ingenious Artist painting
> the *Spring,* talks of a *Snow* of Blossoms, and thereby raises an un-
> expected Picture of *Winter.*
>
> (ch. x)

But an artist both ingenuous and ingenious may raise a true art
of sinking on just such a foundation.

> The churchyard pales are black against the night
> And snow hung here seems doubly white.
>
> ("Night-time in the Cemetery")

Stevie Smith's choice of the noun "pales" for the black railings has an inspired perversity: an antipun, it gives an idea just opposite to what it seemed meant to describe, and it pales into significance.

All these are the figures of speech for someone who, in the words of the Augustan mocker, has "a mind to be simple." Stevie Smith's mind to be simple was subtle with all of them, and with rhythms and rhymes.

"Is there not an Art of *Diving* as well as of *Flying?*" The art of sinking in poetry reaches one of its high (and low) points in her most famous poem.

NOT WAVING BUT DROWNING

Nobody heard him, the dead man,
But still he lay moaning:
I was much further out than you thought
And not waving but drowning.

Poor chap, he always loved larking
And now he's dead
It must have been too cold for him his heart gave way,
They said.

Oh, no no no, it was too cold always
(Still the dead one lay moaning)
I was much too far out all my life
And not waving but drowning.

It is literally about sinking, and its laughter is submarine and profound. Submarine, in the way in which the nouns "wave" and "waves" are forever fended off within the poem and yet are what tacitly corroborates the antithesis of "not waving but drowning"; the likelihood of which is clear from "Death's Ostracism," where "he will call the waves to friend," and from "Mrs. Arbuthnot":

Crying: I should write a poem,
Can I look a wave in the face

> If I do not write a poem about a sea-wave,
> Putting the words in place.

Profound, in that the dead man has not been allowed to die, truly to die.

In her poem about a Roman family, "Tenuous and Precarious." "There was my brother Spurious,/Spurious Posthumous." Spurious Posthumous, because it may be that there is something spurious about the fear—or the hope—that anybody will ever be allowed to become really posthumous; and Spurious Posthumous for the more worldly reasons. There has been something spurious about Stevie Smith's posthumous reputation. In the years since her death in 1971, she has been co-opted into a feminism for which she felt some sympathy but also some distaste; she deplored "the flag-wavers of both sexes," and might have thought that they were not only waving but drowning. She has been playwritten as *Stevie,* her poems and her nature cropped so that she might be plausibly rendered on stage and screen by Glenda Jackson. She has been adapted for a staged anthology. Still, these years have seen the reprinting of her novels, which matters; the publication of a Penguin *Selected Poems,* and of an excellent selection of poetry and prose (by Hermione Lee), which matters more; and the publication of the *Collected Poems,* which matters most. If we are to honor her this side idolatry, the reservations need not only be about her drawings (which are too cute, as Larkin thought), but about the price paid for her unmistakability, her idiosyncrasy. Larkin said of some of the less good poems that "one could never forget when reading one that this was a *Stevie Smith* poem."[24] Yet how good of Stevie Smith to have written so many poems that one could simply never forget.

1984

24. *Observer,* 23 Jan. 1972.

*

A Memorable Voice
Stevie Smith

SEAMUS HEANEY

Always inclined to the brisk definition, W. H. Auden once declared that poetry was memorable speech. The *Collected Poems* of the late Stevie Smith prompt one to revise that: poetry is memorable voice. The unknown quantity in my response to the book was the memory of the poet's own performance of her verse, her voice pitching between querulousness and keening, her quizzical presence at once inviting the audience to yield her their affection and keeping them at bay and a quick irony. She seemed to combine elements of Gretel and of the witch, to be vulnerable and capable, a kind of Home Counties *sean bhean bhocht,* with a hag's wisdom and a girl's wide-eyed curiosity. She chanted her poems artfully off-key, in a beautifully flawed plainsong that suggested two kinds of auditory experience: an embarrassed party-piece by a child half-way between tears and giggles, and a deliberate *faux-naïf* rendition by a virtuoso.

This raises the whole question of poetry for the eye versus poetry for the ear. Perhaps the *versus* is an overstatement, yet there are poets whose work is enhanced and amplified in its power to move once we know the characteristic tone and rhythm and texture of the poet's physical voice. The grave inward melodies of Wallace Stevens become more available if we happen to have heard that Caedmon recording of him reading "The Idea of Order at Key West." Similarly, Robert Frost's words are enlivened by any memory of his switchback pacing, the hard and fluent contours of his accent. And I am sure that Coleridge's excitement on first hearing Wordsworth read was as much a matter of how the poem sounded as of what it intended.

But in the case of Stevie Smith, it is not simply a matter of extra gratification from the poems on the page if we happen to have heard her. It is the whole question of the relationship between a speaking voice, a literary voice (or style), and a style of speech shared by and typical of a certain social and cultural grouping. In other words, it is essential to bring to the appreciation of these poems an ear aware of the longueurs and acerbities, the nuanced understatements and tactical intonations of educated middle-class English speech. The element this work survives in is a disenchanted gentility, and while I can imagine, for example, the Reverend Ian Paisley making a fine job of Yeats's "Under Ben Bulben," I cannot imagine Stevie Smith's idiosyncratic rhythms and meters surviving the hammer-and-tongue of that vigorous North Antrim emphasis.

One is tempted to use worlds like "fey," "arch," and "dotty" when faced with her *Collected Poems* and yet such adjectives sell Stevie Smith's work short. These odd, syncopated, melancholy poems are haunted by the primitive and compelling music of ballad and nursery rhyme, but it has been transposed by a sophisticated and slightly cosseted poetic ear into a still, sad, drawing-room music of humanity, as in "Nor We of Her to Him":

> He said no word of her to us
> Nor we of her to him,
> But oh it saddened us to see
> How wan he grew and thin.
> We said: She eats him day and night
> And draws the blood from him,
> We did not know but said we thought
> This was why he grew thin.

There is variety and inventiveness, much humor and understanding, and a constant poignancy. Her gift was to create a peculiar emotional weather between the words, a sense of pity for what is infringed and unfulfilled, as in the much anthologized "Not Waving but Drowning," or in the following, "Pad, Pad":

I always remember your beautiful flowers
And the beautiful kimono you wore
When you sat on the couch
With that tigerish crouch
And told me you loved me no more.

What I cannot remember is how I felt when you were unkind
All I know is, if you were unkind now I should not mind.
Ah me, the power to feel exaggerated, angry and sad
The years have taken from me, Softly I go now, pad pad.

Stevie Smith reminds you of two Lears: the old king come to knowledge and gentleness through suffering, and the old comic poet Edward veering off into nonsense. I suppose in the end the adjective has to be "eccentric." She looks at the world with a mental squint, there is a disconcerting wobble in the mirror she holds up to nature.

Death, waste, loneliness, cruelty, the maimed, the stupid, the innocent, the trusting—her concerns were central ones, her compassion genuine and her vision almost tragic. Yet finally the voice, the style, the literary resources are not adequate to the somber recognitions, the wounded joie de vivre, the marooned spirit we sense they were destined to express. There is a retreat from resonance, as if the spirit of A. A. Milne successfully vied with the spirit of Emily Dickinson.

The genetic relations which the forms of these poems often bear to the clerihew and the caricature prevent them from attaining the kind of large orchestration that they are always tempting us to listen for. And if they are the real thing when measured by Auden's definition, they miss the absolute intensity required by Emily Dickinson's definition: when you read them, you don't feel that the top of your head has been taken off. Rather, you have been persuaded to keep your head at all costs.

1976

Selected Bibliography

Poetry

A Good Time Was Had by All. London: Jonathan Cape, 1937.
Tender Only to One. London: Jonathan Cape, 1938.
Mother, What Is Man? London: Jonathan Cape, 1942.
Harold's Leap. London: Chapman and Hall, 1950.
Not Waving but Drowning. London: Deutsch, 1957.
Selected Poems. London: Longmans, Green, 1962; New York: New Directions, 1964.
The Frog Prince and Other Poems. London: Longmans, Green, 1966.
The Best Beast. New York: Knopf, 1969.
Scorpion and Other Poems. London: Longmans, Green, 1971.
The Collected Poems of Stevie Smith. London: Allen Lane, 1975, 1978; New York: Oxford Univ. Press, 1974; New Directions, 1983; London: Penguin, 1985.
New Selected Poems. New York: New Directions, 1988.

Novels

Novel on Yellow Paper. London: Jonathan Cape, 1936; New York: Morrow, 1937; Harmondsworth: Penguin, 1951, 1972; New York: Popular Library, 1976; London: Virago, 1980; New York: Pinnacle, 1982.
Over the Frontier. London: Jonathan Cape, 1928, 1958; Virago, 1980; New York: Pinnacle, 1982.
The Holiday. London: Chapman and Hall. 1949; Virago, 1979; New York: Pinnacle, 1982.

Other Books

Some Are More Human Than Others: Sketchbook. London: Gaberbocchus, 1958.

Cats in Colour. Edited and with an introduction by Stevie Smith. London: Batsford, 1959; New York: Viking, 1960.

The Batsford Book of Children's Verse. Edited and with a preface by Stevie Smith. London: Batsford, 1970; reprinted as *The Poet's Garden*. New York: Viking, 1970.

Me Again: Uncollected Writings of Stevie Smith. Edited by Jack Barbera and William McBrien. London: Virago, 1981; New York: Farrar, Straus, and Giroux, 1982; Vintage, 1983.

Secondary Works

Barbera, Jack, William McBrien, and Helen Bajan. *Stevie Smith: A Bibliography.* Westport, Conn.: Meckler, 1987.

Barbera, Jack, and William McBrien. *Stevie: A Biography of Stevie Smith.* London: Heinemann, 1985; New York: Oxford Univ. Press, 1987.

Dick, Kay. *Ivy and Stevie: Ivy Compton-Burnett and Stevie Smith.* London: Duckworth, 1971; Allison and Busby, 1983.

Rankin, Arthur C. *The Poetry of Stevie Smith: Little Girl Lost.* Gerrards Cross, Bucks.: Colin Smythe, 1985.

Spalding, Frances. *Stevie Smith.* London: Faber, 1988; New York: W. W. Norton, 1989.

Sternlicht, Sanford. *Stevie Smith.* Boston: Twayne, 1990.

Index

217

IN SEARCH OF STEVIE SMITH

was composed in 12 on 13 Garamond No. 3 on a Mergenthaler Linotron 202
by Partners Composition;
printed by sheet-fed offset on 60-pound, acid-free Glatfelter Natural Hi Bulk,
Smyth-sewn and bound over binder's boards in Holliston Roxite B,
and notch bound with paper covers
by Braun-Brumfield, Inc.;
with dust jackets and paper covers printed in 2 colors
by Braun-Brumfield, Inc.;
and published by
SYRACUSE UNIVERSITY PRESS
SYRACUSE, NEW YORK 13244-5160